# Club Law and Management

## Revised Edition

## by Philip R Smith

Published by     The Association of Conservative Clubs Ltd.
                 1 Norfolk Row
                 London SE1 7JP

Printed by       Snell Print Ltd.,
                 Yeovil,
                 Somerset BA20 2HP

Disclaimer

Every care is taken in the preparation of this publication, but neither the author nor publishers can accept responsibility for the consequences of any error or omission, however caused.

# Club Law and Management

Revised Edition

by Philip R Smith

# CONTENTS

## 1.0 Foreword

## PART ONE: LAW, REGULATION AND MANAGEMENT
## 2.0 TYPES OF CLUBS
- Introduction
- Unincorporated Clubs
- Industrial and Provident Societies
- Friendly Societies
- Limited Companies

## 3.0 LICENSING ACT 2003 (England and Wales)
- Introduction
- What is a qualifying club?
- How do I apply for a Club Premises Certificate (CPC)?
- What activities does a CPC authorise?
- What information should be included in the Club Operating Schedule?
- What scale does a CPC plan have to be drawn to?
- How long does a CPC remain valid?
- Can a club apply to vary its CPC once granted?
- What form will a CPC take when granted?
- What happens if a club loses its CPC or it is stolen?
- Will a member of the club need to be a Designated Premises Supervisor and obtain a Personal Licence?
- Who has custody of, and is responsible for, a CPC once granted?
- Will door supervisors have to be licensed by the Security Industry Authority (SIA)?
- How do Licensing Authority Officials determine whether a club is established and conducted in good faith?
- Do clubs have a right of appeal against Licensing Authority decisions?
- How will the club's 'permitted hours' be affected?
- What is the position on drinking-up time?
- What powers of inspection and entry to club premises apply under the Licensing Act?
- Can children be admitted to the club?
- Exceptions
- What is meant by 'regulated entertainment'?
- The Live Music Act 2012
- Should clubs take out a Premises Licence as well as a CPC?

## 4.0 LICENSING (SCOTLAND) ACT 2005

## 5.0 BETTING AND GAMBLING IN CLUB PREMISES

- Club Advertising
- Audit Requirements
- Corporation Tax
- VAT and Room Hire
- Honoraria
- Club Wins Important Case at Employment Tribunal: Unfair Dismissal Claim Rejected
- Financial Controls
- Financial Controls Checklist
- Gaming Machine Finance
- Steward's Accommodation and Taxable Benefits
- Council Tax
- National Insurance
- Budgeting

## 7.0 EMPLOYMENT
- Introduction
- Working Time Regulations
- Holiday Pay
- National Minimum Wage
- Statutory Sick Pay
- Notice Periods
- Redundancy
- Maternity Leave
- Standard Maternity Rights
- Time off for Ante-Natal Care
- Length of Maternity Leave
- Maternity Allowance (MA)
- Right to Return
- Additional Maternity Rights
- Statutory Maternity Pay (SMP)
- Additional Maternity Leave (AML)
- Right to return to work after AML
- Paternity Leave
- Standard Paternity Rights
- Length of Paternity Leave
- Statutory Paternity Pay (SPP)
- Parental Leave
- Length of Parental Leave
- Disciplinary and Grievance Procedures
- Stewards

- Recruiting a Steward
- General
- Accident to Paid Employees

## 8.0 HEALTH & SAFETY
- What is Health and Safety at Work?
- Legal requirements

## 9.0 RULES AND REGULATIONS and OTHER LEGISLATION AFFECTING MEMBERS' CLUBS
- Club Rules and Byelaws
- Alteration of Club Rules
- Inter-Affiliation Ticket Scheme
- Rules governing the issue of Inter-Affiliation (IA) Tickets
- Rules governing the admission of Inter-Affiliated Members to Clubs

EQUALITY ACT 2010
- Types of discrimination
- Direct discrimination
- Indirect discrimination
- Victimisation
- Harassment
- Government guidance on fair and equal procedures
- Government guidance on sex equality conditions
- Disability Discrimination
- Data Protection Act 2018
- Introduction
- Data Protection - what is it all about?
- What is a data controller?
- What is personal data?
- I am secretary of a small members club. Will the GDPR apply to us?
- Do we have to register with the Information Commissioners Office?
- Do we have to change our membership application form?
- Do we have to update our website?
- Do we have to complete any other documentation?
- What happens if we lose any members information?
- Can we still send emails to members?
- Should we use 'consent' or 'legitimate interest' as the basis for keeping data?
- What do we do with details of members who have left?

- Is a locked filing cabinet or password protected database containing members' information sufficiently secure for the purposes of the GDPR?
- Can individuals ask to see the information we hold about them?
- What if we process children's information?
- Pubwatch
- Liability for Lost or Stolen Property
- Noise Pollution
  Playing copyright music (recorded or live) in your club

## 10.0 MEETINGS
### Club Meetings: Points of Procedure
- General Meeting
- Notice
- Agenda
- Quorum
- Meeting Chairman
- Validity of Meeting
- Confirmation of Minutes
- Business for which the Meeting was Convened
- Motions
- Amendments
- Voting
- Preparing for an AGM
- Committee Meetings
- A Code of Standing Orders for Committees
- Confidentiality
- General
- Political Meetings
- Sub-Clubs

## PART TWO – 'HOW TO' GUIDES
### A Series of Practical Guides for Those Operating Members' Clubs

### 1.0 How to Control Cash and Stop Staff Theft

CASH CONTROL
- Till systems & cash security
- Basic electronic till
- Pre-set electronic till
- Till opening, operation and closing
- Cash control and staff theft

- Theft of money
- Handling cash
- Staff control

## 2.0 How to Control Stock
- Introduction
- Why is stock taking necessary?
- Ordering stock
- Delivery of stock
- How should a bar's inventory be counted?
- Spirits and wines
- Draught beer, lager, and cider
- Counting full bottles of beer and soft drinks
- Choosing the System
- Inventory Management Systems
- The role of the stocktaker
- How does the 'overage' arise?
- What are the implications of a stock deficit?
- Formula for taking stock
- Storage
- Goods on sale

## 3.0 How to Understand your Club's Finances
- Financial controls
- Accountancy services
- Who requires access to your bookkeeping or accounts?
- What do you need to record?
- Terminology
- Profit & Loss Account (P&L Account)
- Differences between P&L and cashflow
- Profit & Loss Account
- A cashflow forecast
- Actions on the back of cash-flow
- Calculating the sales price and retail price from the cost price

VALUE ADDED TAX
- Introduction
- Calculating VAT returns

## 4.0 How to Do Merchandising, Presentation, and Pricing
- What is merchandising?
- Growing turnover and profits

- The bar or counter
- The farewell
- Building safety and fire safety
- The welcome
- Taking the order
- The farewell

## 6.0 How to Manage the Cellar

### Introduction to the cellar

WHAT IS BEER?
- How is beer made?
- Hygiene
- Temperature
- Stock control and deliveries
- Accepting the delivery
- Best-before dates
- Storing the stock
- Manual handling

CASK ALE
- Introduction to cask ale
- The Stages of conditioning a cask
- Stillaging
- Venting
- Tapping
- Connecting the beer for sale
- Conditioning a cask using 'extractor rods'
- Temperature of cask ales

KEG BEERS
- Introduction to keg beers
- Gases
- Properties of $CO_2$/mixed gas
- Changing a keg
- Fob detectors
- Coolers
- Python

LINE CLEANING AND CHEMICALS
- Introduction to beer-line cleaning
- The line cleaning process

## COSHH
- Control of Substances Hazardous to Health (see Section 9 Health and Safety)

## 7.0 How to Deliver the Perfect Serve
- Introduction
- Lager
- Cask ale and keg beers
- Guinness and other stouts
- Spirits and mixers
- Wines
- Soft drinks
- Coffee

## 8.0 How to Comply with Food Allergens Law

FOOD ALLERGENS
- Introduction
- Rules and legislation
- Allergen rules
- Applicable law
- Important definitions
- Catering establishments
- Pre-packed or loose foods
- Criminal law
- Civil law
- Allergies and their effects in the body
- Definition of a food allergy
- Symptoms of an allergic reaction
- Definition of food intolerance
- Symptoms of food intolerance
- Definition of anaphylactic reaction
- Symptoms of an anaphylactic reaction
- Allergen descriptions
- In the club restaurant
- Which staff are impacted?
- Providing allergen information
- Responsibilities
- Your responsibilities as a club operator
- Customer responsibilities
- Requirement for non-pre-packed and pre-packed for direct sale foods

## 9.0 How to Do Social Media

## 1.0 Foreword

'Club Law & Management' is the natural title to use for this book since it is the heading used for the legal section of the Conservative Clubs Magazine, a section which I have been writing and editing for many years, although much of this work is now undertaken by Charles Littlewood, the ACC's Deputy CEO. The book has not been written exclusively for Conservative Clubs as the information is appropriate for any Private Members' Club operating under a Club Premises Certificate.

In this revised second edition I have introduced a new 'How to' section in Part 2 of the book that goes beyond law and regulation and addresses many of the commercial and financial issues of running a club successfully. They have been written by industry expert Paul Chase. I hope readers will find this helpful in addressing the challenges of operating in an increasingly competitive environment.

All social clubs operate in a much more competitive environment than when I first joined the sector over 30 years ago. They face competition not only from pubs, restaurants, and bars, but also from home entertainment and dining-in opportunities. When clubs recruit new members or seek to retain their existing members, they must be mindful of the fact that today, more than ever before, people have high expectations when they seek food, drink, entertainment and social opportunities outside the home. Social clubs must compete for business with professionally run licensed premises of all types, and this creates the need to up our game.

Social clubs have some unique selling points. They offer value for money; they are run by volunteers who are motivated by community spirit; they offer the opportunity to socialise with like-minded people in an environment that is safe and secure. In the wake of the COVID-19 pandemic this has never been more relevant.

I hope this book will aid the many officers and committee members who devote much of their spare time in taking on the responsibility of managing clubs which play a vital part in our communities.

Thanks go to Paul Chase and Charles Littlewood in assisting with the collating and editing this updated second edition.

Philip Smith
Lord Smith of Hindhead CBE

Philip Smith is the Chief Executive of The Association of Conservative Clubs Limited. He is a Conservative Peer, Party Whip and has served on a number of Select Committees. In addition, he is a Treasurer of The Conservative Party and Chairman of the National Conservative Draws Society. He is also Chairman of the Committee of Registered Clubs' Associations (CORCA) and Chairman of Best Bar None.

# PART ONE: LAW, REGULATION AND MANAGEMENT

## 2.0    TYPES OF CLUBS
### Introduction

Clubs fall into two main categories – those in which the management of the club is in the hands of the members themselves (referred to as 'members' clubs') and those controlled by a proprietor (referred to as 'proprietary clubs'). For the purposes of this book, the subject of members' clubs is dealt with exclusively.

Members' clubs do not carry on a business in their ordinary transactions among members. The supply of drink, food or any other item to members does not constitute a sale since members are paying for a share of stock which they already collectively own.

Therefore, any financial surplus created from the activities of members is not regarded as a profit and is not subject to corporation tax. It is for this reason that members' clubs are sometimes referred to as 'non-profit making clubs'. Such a reference should not be interpreted literally. Clubs must maximise their 'surplus/profits' like any commercial business to sustain and develop their activities. The 'non-profit making' reference merely indicates the mutual trading activities described above.

Members' clubs may be subdivided into several different categories according to their constitution. These include unincorporated members' clubs, clubs incorporated under the Industrial and Provident Societies Acts, clubs registered under the Friendly Societies Acts and clubs incorporated under the Companies Acts.

This chapter sets out the differences between these four types of members' club.

### Unincorporated Clubs

The most common type of members' club is the unincorporated members' club. These are clubs in which the club's property, both real and personal, is vested in several trustees elected or appointed in accordance with the club's rules.

Once they have been selected, trustees must formally be appointed to a club's Trust Deed. Without this act of conveyance taking place, a club's property will not be legally held by trustees. The expense of appointing new trustees to a club's Trust Deed, together with finding suitable or willing candidates to take on this office, has made a number of unincorporated clubs seek incorporation under the Industrial & Provident Societies Acts (see below) or for the trustee responsibilities to be managed by umbrella Associations.

Unincorporated clubs do not achieve corporate status and therefore cannot take or be subject to legal proceedings in the name of the club. Such proceedings can only be made in the names of the trustees acting on behalf of a club.

Trustees are entitled to indemnity against all liability, costs, damages, claims, and demands which are incurred or suffered in connection with any bona fide transaction or activity carried out on behalf of the club. Such indemnification is usually underwritten by the value of the property of a club, its insurance and, depending on a club's rules, special subscriptions raised from among the membership.

It is important for trustees not to act on behalf of a club without proper instruction from a club's committee, or by resolution of the members, or outside the terms of a club's Trust Deed.

### Industrial and Provident Societies

Registration of a club under the Industrial and Provident Societies Act 1965 gives a club the status of a corporate body with the advantages that this status brings: to take or defend legal proceedings in the name of the club; to hold property, both real and personal, as a perpetual corporation instead of through trustees; and to authenticate its acts with a common seal.

The responsibility and authority for administering this Act is vested in the Financial Conduct Authority (FCA), Mutual Societies Registration Department.

A club registered under this Act is required to include the word 'Limited' at the end of its name to indicate the limited financial liability of the club. Members are required to purchase a share in the club which represents the members' sole liability of the club. The value of a share can be as low as 5p.

Unlike a company, shares in clubs registered under the Industrial and Provident Societies Act are usually restricted to one per member. This single shareholding should not be transferable or withdrawable. This ensures that shares cannot be held outside the membership of the club.

Such clubs must also pay an annual fee, make annual returns, and register all rule amendments with the FCA

Whilst the administrative burden of the Industrial and Provident Societies

Act may appear to be greater than that of an unincorporated club, the benefits of corporate status, with the resulting removal of the need for trustees, and the creation of limited liability of members, is a matter which many clubs find attractive.

## Friendly Societies

Since 1992, it has not been possible for clubs to register under the Friendly Societies Act 1974, although many previously registered clubs continue to operate under this Act. The Friendly Societies Acts were previously administered by the Financial Services Authority, but this has now been abolished. Friendly societies, alongside other mutual societies, are now regulated by the Financial Conduct Authority (FCA)

Clubs operating under this Act are required to elect trustees in whom the property of the club is automatically vested. The need to formally register property in the names of trustees is not required. Like clubs registered under the Industrial and Provident Societies Act, clubs registered as Friendly Societies are required to submit annual returns, register rules and amendments, and pay an annual fee to the FCA.

However, the ability to invest funds and pursue certain objects is too restrictive for the purposes of most clubs. I advise clubs registered as Friendly Societies to consider immediate incorporation under the Industrial and Provident Societies Acts. It is relatively simple for such clubs to transfer their registration in this way although it is not obligatory to do so.

## Limited Companies

I would not advise clubs to seek incorporation under the Companies Acts. Whether limited by share or guarantee, the constitution of a company is mostly consistent with that of a club which, as I have described above, operates as a mutual trading association.

A company's memorandum and articles of association are too cumbersome for the purposes of a club's rule book and the administration required by Companies House to operate a company is often too time-consuming for most Club Secretaries.

A club registered under the Companies Acts may, by special resolution, determine to register under the Industrial and Provident Societies Act. The powers to make such a conversion are contained in Section 141 of the Companies Act 1948 and in Section 53 of the Industrial and Provident Societies Act 1965.

A small number of clubs have a situation where their land and buildings are held by companies, which in turn are owned by the club. Such scenarios are usually the result of historic accident and can be the source of confusion caused by share registers not being kept up to date, shares not being properly recorded and Directors not being registered or removed from registration.

Clubs in this situation should seek advice on how to convert both the company and club to registration under the Industrial and Provident Societies Acts. Such conversion would provide one consolidating constitution that would properly serve the objects of the club.

## 3.0    LICENSING ACT 2003 (England and Wales)

### Introduction

Licensing Laws received their first fundamental change for forty years with the introduction of the Licensing Act 2003. The Act applies to England and Wales and does not extend to Scotland.

Whilst many in the social club sector had reservations on whether the decision to transfer licensing management from the Magistrates to Local Authorities was sensible, it is, I believe, worth repeating the statement made in the original Guidance Notes on the Licensing Act 2003, as approved by Parliament:

> *The Secretary of State wishes to emphasise that non-profit making clubs make an important contribution to the life of many communities in England and Wales and bring significant benefits. Their activities also take place on premises to which the public do not generally have access and they operate under codes of discipline applying to members and their guests.*
>
> *In determining what conditions should be included in certificates Licensing Authorities should bear these matters in mind and when considering representations from responsible authorities and interested parties, they should bear in mind that conditions should not be attached to certificates unless they can be demonstrated to be strictly necessary.*
>
> *The indirect costs of conditions will be borne by individual members of the club and cannot be recovered by passing on these costs to the general public as would be the case for commercial enterprises or where a club has chosen to carry on the licensable activities at their premises for the public under the authority of a premises licence.'*

The Licensing Act 2003 amalgamates previous licensing regimes which cover the sale and supply of alcohol, the provision of regulated entertainment and the provision of late-night refreshment and replaces them with a single system.

Club Premises Certificates (CPCs) are not time limited unless requested.

The Act has four main objectives, known as the 'licensing objectives', and all of them are of equal importance:

1. The prevention of crime and disorder
2. Public safety
3. The prevention of public nuisance
4. The protection of children from harm

The Licensing Act 2003 recognises that Private Members' Clubs give rise to different issues for licensing law than commercially run premises selling direct to the public. These clubs are generally organisations where members join for a particular social, sporting, or political purpose. The clubs carry out activities on premises to which public access is restricted and alcohol is supplied other than for profit. For these reasons, the 2003 Act preserves aspects of earlier alcohol licensing law, which applied to 'registered members' clubs,' and affords clubs special treatment outside the normal premises licence arrangements.

Clubs which meet specified criteria set out in the 2003 Act are known as 'qualifying clubs.' Clubs may conduct 'qualifying club activities' on their premises under the authority of a Club Premises Certificate (CPC) issued by the Licensing Authority. CPCs entitle clubs to certain benefits, which include supplying alcohol to members and selling it to guests without the need for any member or employee to hold a personal licence, and clubs are not required to specify a designated premises supervisor. There are more limited rights of entry for the Police and other authorised persons as the premises are considered private and not generally open to the public.

### What is a qualifying club?

To be classified as a qualifying club, several general conditions must be met. These are—

- That under the rules of the club, persons may not be admitted to membership, or be admitted as candidates for membership, to any of the privileges of membership without an interval of at least two days between their nomination for membership and their admission

- That under the rules of the club, those becoming members without prior nomination or application may not be admitted to the privileges of membership without any interval of at least two days between their becoming members and their admission

- That the club is established and conducted in good faith as a club

- That the club has at least twenty-five members

- That alcohol is not supplied to members on the premises unless it is by or on behalf of the club

To qualify as a club authorised to supply alcohol to its members and guests, additional conditions must be met. These are–

- The purchase and supply of alcohol by and for the club is managed by a committee made up of elected members of the club – all aged over 18 years

- No arrangements may be made for any person to receive any commission, percentage, or similar payment at the expense of the club with reference to purchases of alcohol by the club

- No arrangements may be made for any person to derive directly or indirectly any monetary benefit from the supply of alcohol to members or guests apart from to benefit the club as a whole or any indirect benefit a person derives by reason of the supply contributing to a general gain for the club as a whole.

## How do I apply for a Club Premises Certificate (CPC)?

An application for a Club Premises Certificate (CPC) must be made to the relevant licensing authority, that is, the authority within whose area the premises or the major part of the premises is situated.

To make an application, the following must be submitted–

- A completed application form

- An operating schedule

- A plan of the premises in the prescribed form

- A copy of the club's existing Registration Certificate

- A copy of the club's rules

- The appropriate fee

Applications must be advertised as set out in the Act and the Licensing Act 2003 (Premises Licences and Club Premises Certificates) Regulations 2005. This includes displaying a sign at or outside the club premises and an advertisement in a locally circulating newspaper.

## What activities does a CPC authorise?

A CPC may authorise the conduct of any of the qualifying club activities, namely–

- The supply of alcohol by or on behalf of the club to, or to the order of, members of the club

- The retail sale of alcohol by or on behalf of the club to a guest of a member of the club for consumption on the premises where the sale takes place

- The provision of regulated entertainment

You will have to specify in the club operating schedule the qualifying club activities to which the application relates. I would advise all Clubs to request all three activities.

## What information should be included in the Club Operating Schedule?

The club operating schedule is a document in which the club sets out various details in relation to its application for a CPC.

It must include the following information–

- The qualifying club activities to which the application relates

- The proposed hours of those activities and any other times during which it is proposed that the premises are to be open to the members

- Where the relevant qualifying club activities include the supply of alcohol, whether the supplies are for consumption on or off premises or both

- The steps which it is proposed to take to promote the licensing objective, for example the arrangements for door security to promote the prevention of crime and disorder

- Such other information as is required to be included by regulations to be made by the Secretary of State

## What scale does a CPC plan have to be drawn to?

A plan of the premises should be submitted with every application for a CPC.

Each plan must be drawn to a scale of 1:100 and should include the following information–

- The extent of the boundary of the building (if relevant) and any external and internal walls of the building and the perimeter of the premises (if different)

- The location of points of access to and egress from the premises

- The location of escape routes from the premises

- In a case where the premises is used for more than one existing licensable activity, the area within the premises used for each activity

- Fixed structures (including furniture) or similar objects temporarily in a fixed location (but not furniture) which may impact on the ability of individuals on the premises to use exits or escape routes without impediment

- The location of any stage or raised area and the height of each stage or raised area relative to the floor

- The location of any steps, stairs, elevators, or lifts

- The location of any room or rooms containing public conveniences

- The location and type of any fire safety and any other safety equipment, including if applicable, marine safety equipment

- The location of a kitchen, if any, on the premises

## How long does a CPC remain valid?

Until such time as it is withdrawn or surrendered. A CPC may be withdrawn when a club ceases to be a 'qualifying club' e.g., its membership falls below twenty-five, although it can be given three months grace to restore its membership to the required level. Withdrawal is the most extreme penalty a Licensing Authority can impose and is an unusual step resulting from a serious failure of compliance in direct contravention of one of the licensing objectives.

## Can a club apply to vary its CPC once granted?

A club can apply to vary its CPC if it wishes to change the club's opening hours or its qualifying activities. The club would have to advertise its application and pay the appropriate fee. If the application is not opposed by a responsible authority (e.g., the Police, Fire Authority, or other [mainly] enforcement Authorities) or 'other persons' – members of the public – then the application should be granted subject to mandatory licensing conditions and any conditions proposed by the applicant or imposed by the Licensing Authority to promote the licensing objectives. A variation cannot be allowed where a substantial change to the club's premises is involved.

### What form will a CPC take when granted?

The CPC will–

- Specify the name and address of the club
- Include a plan of the premises
- Give the qualifying activities for which the premises may be used
- Specify any conditions to which the CPC is subject
- Be issued to the club with a summary

### What happens if a club loses its CPC or it is stolen?

The club can apply to its Licensing Authority for a copy of the CPC or summary if either is lost, stolen, damaged or destroyed. Loss or theft must be reported to the Police. A fee may be payable to the Licensing Authority.

### Will a member of the club need to be a Designated Premises Supervisor and obtain a Personal Licence?

There is no requirement to have a designated premises supervisor or for a member of the club to be a personal licence holder, or for the club to employ an individual who holds a personal licence, in order for the club to be able to obtain a club certificate to authorise it to sell or supply alcohol. If a qualifying club decides to apply for a premises licence, then it will need to specify an individual to be the designated premises supervisor for its premises and it may only supply alcohol if the supply is made or authorised by a personal licence holder.

### Who has custody of, and is responsible for, a CPC once granted?

The Secretary of the club must ensure that the CPC, or a certified copy, is kept at the club premises in the custody or under the control of a 'nominated person'. A 'nominated person' is one of the following–

- The Secretary

- Any club member
- A person who works for the club at the club premises

A 'nominated person' i.e. someone other than the Secretary, must be nominated for the purpose in writing and notice to that effect given to the Licensing Authority by the Secretary. In other words, the Secretary is automatically deemed to be the custodian of the CPC, unless written confirmation is given by the club to state otherwise.

The 'nominated person' must secure that the summary, or a certified copy, and a notice specifying the position which he/she holds are prominently displayed at the club premises.

## Will door supervisors have to be licensed by the Security Industry Authority (SIA)?

If a qualifying club, under the authorisation of a club premises certificate, decides to have door supervisors for a particular event, there is no mandatory condition in the Licensing Act 2003 that states they will have to be licensed by the Security Industry Authority (SIA).

Persons carrying outdoor management duties for a club i.e. checking membership and Inter-Affiliation Tickets etc. are also not required to be licensed.

A Licensing Authority could impose a condition on a club's CPC that it is necessary for door supervisors to be SIA registered, but this is very rare.

## How do Licensing Authority officials determine whether a club is established and conducted in good faith?

The Licensing Authority will need to look at several matters, including–

- Any arrangements restricting the freedom of the club to purchase alcohol
- Any arrangements where the money or property of the club or any gain arising from the running of the club can be used for purposes otherwise than for the benefit of the club as a whole or for charitable, benevolent, or political purposes
- The arrangements for giving members information about the finances of the club
- The finances or any other accounting records kept to ensure accuracy of that information

- The nature of the premises used by children admitted to the club

## Do clubs have a right of appeal against Licensing Authority decisions?

The Act provides certain rights of appeal to the Magistrates' Court for those who feel aggrieved by decisions made by licensing authority officials. A right of appeal is not only afforded to clubs applying for a CPC where their application has been rejected, or has been granted subject to conditions, but is also afforded to those who made relevant representations in relation to an application.

## How will the club's 'permitted hours' be affected?

Under the Act there are no set 'permitted hours'. Where such a variation in the hours during which the club's conduct of licensable activities is sought, the club will have to set out in the operating schedule the proposed new hours, and these hours will have to be advertised and copied to the relevant 'responsible authorities'.

A licensing authority official may impose restrictions or conditions on requested hours during which licensable activities are carried out, though the terms for making such restrictions are limited. Greater objections are more likely to come from the Police and local residents if the hours requested are excessive. A hearing and appeals procedure are available if differences cannot be reconciled.

I would advise clubs to ask for longer trading hours than would normally be needed on a regular basis, thereby providing a degree of flexibility and avoiding the cost and administration of altering the operating schedule on every occasion an extension is required, but not to go so far as to request extended hours which are likely to attract objections.

Of course, the extent to which trading hours will be extended is ultimately determined by local market conditions. Members only have a finite amount of money to spend, and clubs only have a finite amount of money for paying club employees to work during these extra hours.

## What is the position on drinking-up time?

The Licensing Act 2003 does not lay down any statutory limits on opening hours and is silent about drinking-up time. Clubs are therefore free to set out their proposed hours for conducting licensable activities, such as the sale of alcohol and the provision of entertainment, and of their general opening and closing times, in their CPC applications and operating schedules.

The consumption of alcohol is not a licensable activity under the 2003 Act; it is the sale or supply of alcohol that is licensable. The concept of 'drinking-up time' under the Licensing Act 1964 no longer applies and consumption of alcohol can take place at any time the club is open, but sale or supply of alcohol may be subject to different start and finish times. A club's operating schedule should state the times that licensable activities will take place on the premises, including the time at which they will stop, and it is sensible to state a time at which the premises will close that is later than the termination time for licensable activities such as the sale or supply of alcohol or the provision of regulated entertainment.

### What powers of inspection and entry to club premises apply under the Licensing Act?

Where a club applies for a CPC or a variation of an existing CPC, or an application is made to the licensing authority for a review of a CPC, an authorised person (i.e. a licensing authority official, a fire officer, a Health and Safety Executive Inspector etc.) or a Constable may, on production of his authority enter and inspect the premises. Forty-eight hours' notice must be given to the club and the inspection should take place within fourteen days after the making of the relevant application (i.e. for a CPC, a variation of CPC or a review of a CPC). Obstruction of an authorised person or Constable undertaking an inspection is an offence.

A Constable may enter and search club premises operating under a CPC if he has reasonable cause to believe that an offence under Section 4(3) (a)(b) or (c) of the Misuse of Drugs Act 1971 is being, or is about to be, committed or if a breach of the peace is likely.

### Can children be admitted to the club?

Persons less than 18 years of age may be admitted to the club but children less than 16 must be accompanied by a parent or other responsible person of at least 18 years of age. It is an offence for a person less than 18 to be supplied with intoxicating liquor in a Registered Private Members' Club.

The following are offences under the Act–

- Sale of alcohol to a person less than 18 years of age
- Supply of alcohol to a club member less than 18 years of age

- Purchasing alcohol when less than 18 years of age
- Purchasing alcohol on behalf of a person less than 18
- Consuming alcohol when less than 18 years of age
- Sending an individual less than 18 years of age to obtain alcohol

## Exceptions

The exception to the age restrictions listed above is that consumption of beer, cider, wine or perry by a person aged 16 or 17 years is permitted with a meal, provided the alcohol is purchased by a person aged at least 18 years and the 16 or 17-year-old is accompanied at the meal by a person aged at least 18.

## What is meant by 'regulated entertainment'?

A wide range of entertainment is included in the Act and regulated entertainments are defined as–

- A performance of live music
- Any playing of recorded music
- A performance of a play
- An exhibition of a film
- A performance of dance
- An indoor sporting event
- Boxing or wrestling entertainment
- Entertainment of a similar description where the entertainment takes place in the presence of an audience and is provided for the purpose of entertaining that audience.

Also included is the provision of 'entertainment facilities', which means providing facilities for making music and for dancing. 'Entertainment facilities' are, for example, a dance floor provided for customers to use, whereas 'entertainment' might involve a performance of dance provided for an audience.

For the provision of entertainment or entertainment facilities to be regulated, two conditions must be satisfied–

- The first of these, so far as clubs are concerned, is that the entertainment facilities must be provided exclusively for members and their guests of a club which is a qualifying club in relation to the provision of regulated entertainment

- The second is that the premises on which the entertainment takes place or entertainment facilities provided are made available for the entertainment to take place

All clubs will qualify under the second point, which means that the entertainment is properly authorised by the club.

## The Live Music Act 2012

In 2012 a significant change was introduced regarding the provision of regulated entertainment in respect of premises authorised to sell or supply alcohol under a club premises certificate or premises licence. The Live Music Act 2012 changes some key fundamentals:

- It removes the requirement for a licensing permission for unamplified live music between the hours of 08.00 and 23.00 to audiences of any size

- It removes the requirement for a licensing permission for amplified live music between the hours 08.00 and 23.00 to audiences of no more than 500

- In 2015 these deregulatory changes were also applied to recorded music

- As these activities will no longer be considered licensable activities, any existing conditions on the CPC or premises licence which refer specifically to live or recorded music between 08.00 and 23.00 will be disapplied

- You do not need to apply to your Licensing authority to amend your CPC, the conditions simply no longer apply, although it is possible for a Licensing Authority to impose conditions regarding entertainment during these times in the event of a review of the CPC following a complaint about noise nuisance

The Live Music Act does not remove the requirement for permission to play live and recorded music from PPL and PRS for Music. These two copyright organisations have now formed a joint venture to simplify getting permission to play copyright music to the public. Clubs no longer need to make separate applications to PPL and PRS for Music. Under the joint venture there is one application made for what is called 'The Music Licence'.

## Should clubs take out a Premises Licence as well as a CPC?

Generally, I would not recommend this course of action. Clubs which wish to operate a commercial venture in respect of providing facilities for the public would need to hold these two separate forms of licensing permission. A club would become divided between activities run for members and commercial activities run for non-members. Not only will this create difficulty with accounting, since income derived from outside the membership is subject to Corporation Tax, but the possession of a Premises Licence involves a great deal more regulation and red tape than the operation of a CPC.

## Sales of Drink to Non-Members

The subject of non-member activities within Registered Private Members' Clubs is one which has become increasingly important, since almost all clubs now rely to a greater or lesser extent, on income generated from the sales of drink at private functions promoted by either individual members or outside organisations.

The most interesting change introduced by the 2003 Act is that members' guests introduced on a normal day-to-day basis will be permitted to purchase drinks. While in practice this has been accepted in many clubs, strictly speaking the previous rules of almost all clubs prevented such sales.

Consequently, drink may be supplied lawfully to a non-member attending any event promoted by a member, provided the non-member is a bona fide guest of the member and has been properly admitted to the club in accordance with the club's rules.

Any member wishing to hold a private function or party in their club will be able to do so and the number of functions is not restricted in number. Naturally, if a person who is not a member approaches a club with a request to hire a room in order to hold a private function, then the club could legitimately ask if the person would like to become a member. Provided such persons met the membership requirements of the club's rules, their election to membership would automatically make the event a members' private function at which his or her guests could be lawfully supplied with drink.

The rules of almost every club put no restriction on the number of guests a member may introduce at any one time but do, rightly, restrict the number of occasions the same guest may be introduced in any one month.

The Act contains no reference to the way in which clubs should manage the introduction of guests and no reference to the number of members' functions or parties which could be held. Such functions would, of course, have to be booked and the committee would retain ultimate discretion on whether to agree to a booking, or not.

Therefore, do not accept any criticism or suggested rule amendments concerning this matter from either Licensing Authorities or Police licensing officers, and refer any such matters to your affiliated organisation. I have seen some examples of ridiculous suggested rule amendments being passed off as 'legal requirements' by Licensing Authority officials; all these suggestions have been withdrawn on being challenged.

## Temporary Event Notices (TENs)

Part 5 of the 2003 Act makes provision for a system that would allow individuals known as 'premises users' to carry out licensable activities on a temporary basis (for a period not exceeding 168 hours), subject to various conditions and limits attaching to the number of events that may be permitted. Different limits apply depending on whether the person carrying out licensable activities holds a personal licence and the frequency of use of the premises.

## Important definitions

*Premises user' means:*
A person aged at least 18 years who issues a temporary event notice.

*Temporary activity' means:*
A 'permitted temporary activity' is one that is carried on in accordance with a temporary
event notice given to the relevant licensing authority and which satisfies certain conditions.

*Temporary event notice (TEN)' means:*
A notice submitted to the licensing authority by a premises user who proposes to carry on a licensable activity for a temporary period of not more than 168 hours. Such a notice is defined as a 'temporary event notice'. The 'premises user' must be at least 18 years old.

Examples
- For personal licence holders, the number of occasions which could

be covered by these arrangements in any one calendar year would be subject to a limit of 50

- Where an individual who does not hold a personal licence, such as the club secretary, wishes to carry out one or more licensable activities at the premises, regardless of whether they are covered by a premises licence relating to those activities, this may be done by the same person on no more than five occasions in any one calendar year.

- In both cases, the arrangements would only apply where the number attending the event is no more than 499 people at any point in time. In addition, no premises may be used for temporary events on more than 15 occasions, stretching over an overall maximum of 21 days in any one calendar year.

## Conditions for a temporary event

- The temporary event notice has been duly acknowledged by the licensing authority and notified to the police and environmental health

- The temporary event notice has not been subsequently withdrawn by the individual giving the notice

- The licensing authority has not issued a counter-notice. A counter notice would be issued following a hearing of any objections raised by the police or environmental health authority to the effect that any of the licensing objectives would be undermined by allowing the activity to go ahead or if the permitted limits to the person giving the notice or to the premises would be exceeded

## Details about a temporary event to be included in the TEN

- The licensable activities that are to be carried out

- The total length of the event - which must not exceed 168 hours

- The times during the event that the licensable activities are to be carried out (e.g., where an individual wants to organise an event that covers 36 hours and where the bar will be open for two evenings within that time)

- The maximum number of people to be allowed on to the premises at any one time, which must be no more than 499

- Whether any alcohol sales are to be made for consumption on or off the premises (or both)

- Any other information that may be prescribed by regulations

## Notice periods and police and environmental health authorities' objections

TENs must be issued to the local licensing authority and notified to the police and environmental health authority and both have the right to object, and all the licensing objectives can be engaged by an objection.

There are two types of TEN:

- a standard TEN - given no less than 10 working days' notice before the event, and

- a late TEN - given no earlier than 9 days and not later than five days before the event

- If you hold a personal licence you can issue up to 10 late TENs a year; if you don't, up to two.

Before the time of the event the licensing authority must:

- Acknowledge the notice

- The police and environmental health authority must consider the notice and decide whether to give notice of objection

If the police or environmental health object the licensing authority must, if necessary, convene a hearing to decide whether to issue a counter notice. The temporary event notice must be submitted in duplicate and accompanied by the fee. The premises user must give a copy of any temporary event notice to:

- The chief officer of police and environmental health authority for the area no later than 10 working days before the event is due to begin. TENs submitted less than 10 days but at least 5 working days can be accepted unless the police or environmental health authority object

- Where the police or environmental health are satisfied that allowing the premises to be used for a temporary event would undermine any of the licensing objectives, they must issue an 'objection notice' stating the reasons why they believes the temporary event would undermine the licensing objectives and which objectives are engaged by the application

- The objection notice must be given no later than 48 hours after the chief officer of police and environmental health is given the temporary event notice and is sent to the relevant licensing authority and the premises user.

## Police and Environmental Health objections and the issuing of a counter-notice

Where there is an objection to a temporary event notice, the licensing authority must:

- Hold a hearing to consider the objection notice unless all parties agree that a hearing is unnecessary

- If the authority accepts the objection it must issue a 'counter-notice' to the premise's user in which case the event cannot proceed

- If the authority does not accept the objection it must inform the police or EHA

- Any decision or counter-notice must be issued to the premise's user at least 24 hours before the specified event period. A failure to do so will result in the premises user being able to proceed with the event

## Modifying a temporary event notice

- Section 106 of the Act provides that where the authorities have given an objection notice, at any point between notification and the hearing, the authorities and the premises user may agree to modify the temporary event notice in order that it no longer undermines the relevant licensing objective

- When temporary event notices are modified in this way, the objection notice is withdrawn, and the temporary event notice has effect

## Visiting Teams

Some clubs have used rules which permit members and supporters of visiting teams from other clubs and organisations to make use of a club's facilities when participating in organised sporting or other activities.

The Act makes no specific provision for such activities and therefore visiting teams and their supporters will need to be signed in by the host members as their guests. Once signed in as members' guests, they may lawfully be supplied with drink. If the visiting teams are from other affiliated clubs then hopefully, they will have already purchased affiliation tickets, in which case they can enter the club and sign in their own guests in accordance with the host club's rules.

## CPC Fees

Whilst there is no specific renewal date of a CPC in the same way as the previous Registration Certificates, it is necessary for an annual fee to be paid to local Licensing Authority Officials for the CPC to remain in force. Therefore, look out for any renewal invoice received from your local Licensing Authority and ensure that it is paid promptly.

| Rateable value | Band | Initial Fee | Annual Fee |
|---|---|---|---|
| No rateable value to £4,300 | A | £100 | £70 |
| £4,300 to £33,000 | B | £190 | £180 |
| £33,001 to £87,000 | C | £315 | £295 |
| £87,001 to £125,000 | D | £450 | £320 |
| £125,001 and above | E | £635 | £350 |

A multiplier will be applied to premises in Bands D and E where they are used exclusively or primarily for the supply of alcohol for consumption on the premises, as follows-

Band D Initial Fee of £450 x 2 = £900. Annual Fee of 635 x 3 = £1,905.

Band E Initial Fee of £320 x 2 = £640. Annual Fee of £350 x 3 = £1,050.

Since almost all Conservative clubs have a substantial food and entertainment's offering, the multiplier should not apply.

## 4.0 LICENSING (SCOTLAND) ACT 2005

### Background

For over a hundred years, until the Licensing (Scotland) Act 2005 (LSA 2005) came into force on 1 September 2009, private members' clubs in Scotland were not 'licensed' in the sense that a pub or bar is licensed. Instead, they occupied a special position outside of the mainstream licensing system with the ability to supply alcohol resting on a certificate of registration granted by the Sheriff. In fact, alcohol wasn't 'sold', rather, the alcohol stock was treated as the property of the club's members, and it was supplied on the payment of cash over the bar into the club's funds to preserve equity between members who would drink differing amounts.

Under the Licensing (Scotland) Act 1976 Members Clubs were authorised to sell alcohol by means of a Certificate of Registration granted by a Sheriff. Many members' clubs also had regular extensions of permitted hours granted annually by their local Licensing Board. The Licensing (Scotland) Act 2005 brings members clubs which have traditionally been registered with the Sheriff wholly under the remit of their local Licensing Board.

Under the LSA 2005, from 1 September 2009, clubs have been required to hold a premises licence issued by their local Licensing Board. Clubs have become subject to similar regulation to other licensed premises. For example, the Council's Licensing Standards Officer has statutory power to enter licensed premises, including club premises, for the purposes of inspection and examination of records. However, if clubs satisfy certain criteria, special provisions of the Act ensure that some of the requirements of the Act will not apply to their premises

Now, the arrangements under the LSA 2005 mean that clubs can operate in one of two ways – but both require to be the subject of a premises licence issued by the local licensing board.

A club might choose to operate as a:

- 'Qualifying Club': that is, a club that is governed by a constitution and rules meeting certain requirements. These clubs enjoy certain privileges, for example:

    - there is no need to have a designated premises manager, but all staff selling alcohol must nevertheless undergo a minimum of two-hours training as prescribed by regulations

    - overprovision as a ground for refusal is disapplied and the annual licence fee is just £180.

- Other clubs choose to trade on a wholly commercial basis without these advantages. But no matter the type of club, it must sell alcohol and conduct its activities in accordance with the premises licence like any other outlet.


**Definition of Club**

The special provisions of the Act relating to members clubs apply to any Club which:

Is not constituted for the purposes of making a profit; and has a written constitution and rules which make the following provisions:

- The business of the club is under the management of a committee or other governing body elected by the members of the club

-  No person under 18 is to be admitted as a member of the club (unless the club is devoted primarily to some sporting purpose or is a students' union as defined in the regulations)

- No member of the committee or governing body and no employee of the club has any personal interest in the sale of alcohol on the premises or in the profits arising from such sale

- Apart from when an occasional licence has effect on the club premises, no person is to be supplied with alcohol on the club premises unless that person is a member of the club or a guest of a member accompanied by that member, or is a member of another club as defined in the Act

- Where no occasional licence is in force and a person who is on the premises at the invitation of a member of the club and is accompanied by that member is supplied with alcohol, there is to be entered in a book kept for the purpose –

    - The date of supply

    - The name and address of the guest supplied with alcohol; and

    - The name of the member accompanying the person

    - Correct accounts and books are to be kept showing the financial affairs and intromissions of the club

    - The club is to have at least 25 members to be properly constituted, and

    - No person is to be allowed honorary or temporary membership of the club or to be relieved of the payment of the regular entrance fee or subscription, except to allow temporary participation in the activity which is the prime purpose of the club, and except in accordance with specific provisions set out in the club rules.

Members Clubs will be asked on applying to the Licensing Board to certify whether they comply with the above criteria to benefit from the exemptions detailed below. Where such a certification is made, the Members Club will be required to submit a copy of their written constitution and rules to the

Board. Clubs which do not conform to the above criteria will be treated as licensed premises and will not benefit from the exemptions for licensed clubs.

On initial application, Members Clubs will be required to provide details of 'Connected Persons'. Under the Act a Connected Person is defined as an office bearer of the club. There is further requirement for any Connected Person to declare any relevant or foreign conviction which is not spent in terms of the Rehabilitation of Offenders Act 1974.

Clubs must keep their constitutions updated and when revised, submit a copy of the revised constitution to the Clerk to the Licensing Board. Clubs must also ensure their constitution, accounts and entry book are available for inspection by the Licensing Standards Officers and the Police at all reasonable times.

### Lodging an Application for a Premises Licence

Applicants are required to submit the following:

- Premises application
- Operating plan
- Layout plan
- Application fee of £200
- Certificates from Building Standards, Planning and Food Hygiene where food is to be supplied on the premises
- Copy constitution and rules.

The form of the application is prescribed in the Premises Licence (Scotland) Regulations 2007. A copy of the application form and operating plan can be downloaded from the website of any Scottish Licensing Board.

### Access by Children (persons less than 16 years old) and Young Persons (16 & 17) to Clubs

The provisions for allowing children into Members Clubs will follow the same arrangements as other licensed premises under the Act which require such premises to specify in their operating plan whether it is proposed that children and young persons are to be permitted entry to the premises. Where such a proposal is made, the premises will be required to specify the terms on which it is proposed that children and young persons are permitted entry, the times at which they would be allowed on the premises, the ages of such children and the parts of the premises to which they would be permitted access. Appropriate conditions relating to access by children may be attached by the Licensing Board.

## What are the Exemptions for Qualifying Clubs?

Section 125 of the Licensing (Scotland) Act 2005 provides for exemptions from parts of the Act for clubs that fall within the description above. Qualifying Clubs are exempted from:

- The assessments of overprovision (section 7)

- The ground of refusal of an application for premises licence or premises licence variation relating to overprovision (section 23(5)(e) & 30(5)(d))

- The requirement for the operating plan to contain information as to the designated premises manager (section 20(4)(g)) because a DPM is not required

- The requirement for the name and address of the designated premises manager to be specified in the premises licence (section 26(2)(a)(ii))

- The requirement for there to be a designated premises manager for licensed premises (schedule 3 Para 4)

- The requirement for sales of alcohol under the premises licence to be authorised by a personal licence holder (schedule 3 Para 5)

- The requirement for sales of alcohol under certain occasional licences to be authorised by a personal licence holder (schedule 4 Para 4)

These exemptions mean that qualifying clubs will not generally need a personal licence holder or a designated premises manager. The exception is where they open later than 01:00 a.m. and satisfy certain other requirements in which case they may become subject to specific mandatory conditions that include the presence of a personal licence holder.

## What are the training requirements?

The Premises Licence Mandatory Conditions Regulations contained in Schedule 3 to the Act provide at paragraph 6 for the training of all staff selling or serving alcohol unless they hold a personal licence. There is no exemption for clubs from this provision and clubs cannot use untrained staff. Where a person undertakes the role of selling or serving alcohol then that person must be trained to the standard prescribed in the Licensing (Training of Staff) (Scotland) Regulations 2007. That standard is a minimum of two hours' relevant training from a person who holds a personal licence or who is accredited by the Scottish Qualifications Authority (Regulatory).

Many club representatives have undergone recognised training in the past. Certain clubs may therefore choose to have one (or more) personal licence holders even though there is no requirement for Clubs to have personal licence holders. Remember, only personal licence holders can train bar staff. It is recommended that clubs take legal advice on training from their solicitor, from a trade association or from accredited training providers.

Although the Licensing Boards recognise there is no legal requirement for a personal licence holder, many Licensing Boards consider that there are advantages to clubs in employing one and encourage club committees to consider this.

## Occasional Licences and Clubs

In terms of the Licensing (Clubs) (Scotland) Regulations 2007 Members Clubs can apply for and be granted an occasional licence in respect of their licensed premises. This is irrespective of the terms of the normal rule that an occasional licence cannot be granted in respect of licensed premises. This provision was introduced to allow club premises to admit members of the public and sell alcohol to them. The Regulations provide that in respect of such premises the Licensing Board may issue in any 12-month period no more than:

- Four occasional licences each having effect for a period of four days or more; and no more than 12 occasional licences, each having effect for a period of less than four days provided that the total number of days in any period of 12 months in respect of which an occasional licence has effect does not exceed 56.

- When an occasional licence is in force, a club will be able to admit and sell or serve alcohol to members of the general public, as well as members and guests. During this time there will be no requirement for alcohol sales to be authorised by a personal licence holder and no requirement for guests to be signed in by members. Applications for occasional licences must be made to the Board at least six weeks prior to the first date on which the occasional licence is to be in force.

Clubs will appreciate that where they obtain occasional licences so that they can admit and sell/serve alcohol to the public, Licensing Boards will deal with the application in the same manner as it would an application from any commercial organisation.

## 5.0 BETTING AND GAMBLING IN CLUB PREMISES

### Betting

Betting in a registered club is not illegal provided only members are involved, e.g., two members bet £5 on the outcome of the club's talent show. Betting is illegal when non-members are involved or where the club premises are used for betting transactions which are illegal, e.g., with betting operators.

Since 1 September 2007 and the coming into force of the Gambling Act 2005, betting is regulated by the Gambling Commission. All bookmakers are required to have an operating licence from the Gambling Commission. In addition to an operating licence, each individual gambling premises requires a premises licence from their local licensing authority. Such licences are likely to contain requirements for premises holders about their responsibilities not only in relation to the proper conduct of betting but also the protection of children and vulnerable persons, in particular club committees, therefore, are recommended to refuse membership to bookmakers and ensure that they or their agents do not conduct their business on club premises.

### Gambling Act 2005

The Gambling Act 2005 came into force on 1 September 2007.

Under the Gambling Act 2005 the Gambling Commission regulates gambling in Great Britain and arrangements have been introduced to regulate gambling, including bingo, gaming machines and card games, to:

- keep crime out of gambling
- ensure gambling is conducted in a fair and open way, and
- protect children and vulnerable people from being harmed or exploited by gambling.

This will happen through a system of licence conditions and codes of practice for licences and permit holders. The Commission's enforcement officers, as well as police officers, have powers of entry into premises at any time without a warrant for the purposes of inspecting gambling where gambling offences are suspected. Local authority officers have powers of entry when considering an application for a permit.

## Gaming Machine Permits

Under the Act if you operate gambling from your club, it is likely that you will need a permit. Club gaming permits and club machine permits allow the provision of no more than three gaming machines, from categories B3A, B4, C or D.

A club gaming permit allows additional gaming entitlements. Please note all gambling activities will be subject to any conditions or restrictions arising from the 2005 Act and regulations made under it.

## Licences

Under the Act there are three different types of licences that operators may need. They are-

- Operating licences
- Personal licences
- Premises licences

## Operating licences

In some circumstances if you plan to provide facilities for gambling in a member's club, a commercial club, or a miners' welfare institute you may need an operating licence. You may need an operating licence if you provide bingo or other gambling over set limits as outlined. Members' clubs, commercial clubs and miners' welfare institutes can provide some gambling without an operating licence.

## Personal licences

The Act allows exemptions for clubs so that the officers do not need to hold personal licences.

## Premises licences

No premises licence is needed if the club's gambling activities comply with the Act if you play highturnover bingo as explained below.

## VAT

Since 1 November 1975, the net take of the proceeds of gaming machines has been subject to VAT at the standard rate. 'Net take' means the sum of money inserted into machines by players less the winnings paid out i.e. the net proceeds allocated to club funds.

Customs and Excise Officers have access to club premises to inspect them and VAT records. If an officer believes an offence has been committed, he must obtain a magistrate's warrant should he wish to search the premises or any person or records.

### New permits

There are two kinds of club permits under the Act:

- The club machine permit, and

- The club gaming permit

### Club machine permit

The club machine permit enables clubs to offer up to three gaming machines. It does not authorise the provision of any other facilities for gaming (but see exempt gaming below). Club machine permits last for 10 years except where a permit is granted under the fast-track procedure to a club with a club premises certificate (CPC) and then it will last indefinitely.

The law establishes several categories of gaming machines. It restricts the gaming machines that can be operated in a club to categories B3A, B4, C and D.

| Machine Category | Maximum Stake | Maximum Prize |
|---|---|---|
| B3A | £2 | £500 |
| B4 | £1 | £400 |
| C | £1 | £100 |
| D | 10p if money prize is available<br>30p if non-monetary prize is available | £5 money prize<br>£8 non-monetary prize |

All Group D machines are exempt from machine games duty (MGD). Machines dispensing pull-tab tickets are not gaming machines. The use of these machines is subject to certain statutory conditions, and the holder of the permit must comply with the Gambling Commission's Code of Practice on the location and operation of gaming machines. Briefly, permit holders will need to comply with the following provisions, or their permit could be revoked:

- All gaming machines situated on the premises must be located in a place within the premises so that their use can be supervised, either by staff whose duties include such supervision (including bar or floor staff) or by other means

- Permit holders must have in place arrangements for such supervision

- All gaming machines situated on the premises shall be located in a place that requires a customer who wishes to use any ATM made available on the premises to cease gambling at the gaming machine in order to do so

- 'ATM' means a machine located on the premise that enables the person using it to obtain cash by use of a credit or debit card

The Code of Practice also recommends the following best practice should be implemented by permit holders, as below.

## Club gaming permit

The club gaming permit enables clubs to offer up to:

- Three gaming machines, plus

- Facilities for equal chance gaming (subject to certain conditions), a

- Two bankers' games: pontoon and chemin de fer (not blackjack), and

- The permit holder can charge higher participation fees (up to £3 plus VAT per person per day and up to £20 plus VAT for bridge and/or whist)

In addition, gaming in a club or institute that holds a club gaming permit is not subject to the stake a prize limits that apply to exempt gaming.

- There are no limits on stakes and prizes in respect of poker with a club gaming permit

- Club gaming permits also allow clubs to provide a total of 3 gaming machines (categories B3A, B4, C and D)

- Once again, the duration of the permit is for 10 years except where a permit is granted under the fast-track procedure to a club with a club premises certificate (CPC) and then it will last indefinitely

The use of these machines is subject to certain statutory conditions and the holder of the permit must comply with the Gambling Commission's Code of Practice on the location and operation of gaming machines as mentioned above.

You may obtain further information from the Gambling Commission's website. A club can apply to its local licensing authority for either a club machine permit or a club gaming permit (see below). However, no licence or permit is required for clubs that operate solely under the exempt gaming provisions (referred to later).

## Machine Games Duty (MGD)

Machine Games Duty (MGD) is charged on the net takings from the playing of machine games. These are games where customers pay to play a game on a machine in the hope of winning a prize which is greater than the cost to play. Where MGD is payable, it will replace both Amusement Machine Licence Duty (AMLD) and VAT on games played on machines. The current rates of duty can be found at the government's website.

## Exempt gaming

Section 269 of the Act allows clubs (including clubs established and conducted for the purposes of gaming and which otherwise meet the requirements for a members' or a commercial club) to provide certain facilities for gaming without the need for a licence or a permit. In order to qualify for this exemption, the gaming must meet several conditions:

- It must be equal chance gaming, examples would be bingo, bridge and certain poker games

- Stakes and prizes must comply with any limits sets in regulations

- The club must not deduct any amounts from sums staked or won

- Any charge for participation must not exceed amount set by the Secretary of State

- The games played may only take place at one set of premises, so there may not be any linking of games between premises, and

- In the case of members' clubs and miners' welfare institutes only, people may only participate in the gaming if they have been a member (or applied or are nominated for membership) at least 48 hours before playing, or a genuine guest of such a person

**Limits on stakes and prizes for exempt gaming**

- There are at present no limits in the legislation for stakes and prizes for most types of gaming in clubs, however it should be noted that the exempt gaming provisions are intended to facilitate low stakes, low scale gaming activity

- Clubs should therefore take steps to ensure that any gaming permitted on club premises remains at a low level

- There are, however, regulations setting limits on poker played in all clubs under the Exempt Gaming Provisions:

  - There is a stake limit of £10 per player per game (i.e. the limit applies to a game of poker, not a single hand), as well as aggregate stakes limits of £250 per day and £1000 per week for each individual club.

  - Participants must be bona fide club members or guests. For example, a club could run a poker game for 25 players playing £10 each, four times per week. The maximum prize in a game of poker is also £250

  - Where clubs operate under the exempt gaming provisions, they may make a charge of up to £1 per person per day for participation in gaming (£18 Bridge and/or whist).

**Access to gambling by children and young persons**

- Permit holders should put into effect procedures intended to prevent underage gambling. Only members and their guests may play the machines, under 18s may not.

This should include procedures for:

- Checking the age of apparently underage customers; and

- Refusing access to anyone who appears to be underage, and who tries to use category B or C gaming machines and cannot produce an acceptable form of identification

Permit holders should take all reasonable steps to ensure that all relevant employees understand their responsibilities for preventing underage gambling.

Permit holders should only accept identification which:

- Contains a photograph from which the individual can be identified

- Is valid; and

- Is legible and has no visible signs of tampering or reproduction

- Identification is that carrying the PASS logo and hologram, e.g., Citizencard, driving licence (including provisional licence) with photocard, and passport.

Procedures should be in place for dealing with cases where a child or young person repeatedly attempts to gamble on category B or C machines, including oral warnings, reporting the offence to the Gambling Commission and the police and making available information on problem gambling.

## Self-exclusion

This section sets out the best practice which the Gambling Commission considers should be implemented by permit-holders. Compliance with the provision is not a condition of the permit.

These provisions are applicable to club gaming and club machine permit holders. Permit holders should put in place procedures for self-exclusion and take all reasonable steps to refuse service or to otherwise prevent an individual who has entered a self-exclusion agreement from participating in gambling.

Permit holders should implement procedures designed to ensure that an individual who is self-excluded cannot gain access to gambling; these include:

- A register of those excluded with appropriate records

- Photo identification

- Staff training to ensure that relevant staff can enforce the systems, and

- Removal of those self-excluded persons found in the gambling area or attempting to gamble from the premises

Permit holders should take all reasonable steps to ensure that:

- The self-exclusion period is a minimum of six months and gives customers the option of extending this to a total of five years

- Where a customer chooses not to renew and makes a positive request to begin gambling again, then the customer should be given one day to cool off before being allowed access to the gambling facilities

The Gambling Commission does not require the permit holder to carry out an assessment or make any judgment on whether the individual should have access to gambling. The requirement to take positive action in person or over the telephone is purely to check that the customer has considered the decision to access gambling again and allow them to consider the implications, and implement the one-day cooling-off period and explain why this has been put in place.

## Lotteries

A Lottery is defined as a scheme for distributing prizes by lot or chance. All raffles, draws, sweepstakes, totes, or other lotteries by any other name, are declared illegal except for Small Lotteries (incidental to exempt entertainments), Private Society Lotteries, Small Society Lotteries, and the National Lottery.

### Small Lotteries (Incidental to Exempt Entertainments)

To promote such lotteries the following conditions must be observed–

- The entertainments concerned are bazaars, sales of work, fetes, dinners, dances, sporting or athletic events and other entertainments of a similar character

- The whole proceeds of the entertainment (including the proceeds of the lottery) shall be devoted to purposes other than private gain, however, the following may be deducted–

  - The expenses of the entertainment, excluding expenses incurred in connection with the lottery

  - The expenses incurred in printing tickets in the lottery

  - A sum not exceeding £250 that the promoters of the lottery think fit to spend in purchasing prizes in the lottery

- None of the prizes in the lottery shall be money prizes

- Tickets or chances in the lottery shall not be sold or issued, nor shall the result of the lottery be declared, except on the premises on which the entertainment takes place and during the progress of the entertainment

- The facilities afforded for participating in lotteries shall not be the only inducement to persons to attend the entertainment

## Private Society Lotteries

To promote such lotteries the following conditions must be observed–

- The sale of tickets or chances must be confined to members of one society established and conducted for purposes not connected with gaming, betting, or lotteries

- The expression 'society' includes a club, institution, organisation or other association of persons by whatever name called and each society is regarded as separate and distinct; thus two or more clubs cannot combine to hold a joint lottery, which would preclude a federation of clubs from running such a lottery

- The word 'ticket' includes any document issued which entitles the holder to participate in the lottery

- The lottery must be promoted for the club, and the sale of tickets or chances must be confined solely to its members, and to any other persons on the club's premises i.e. members' guests, visitors admitted in accordance with the approved rules, and affiliation ticket holders

- The lottery must be authorised in writing by the club committee, and duly recorded in the Minute book

- The committee must appoint the Secretary or a member of the club to act as 'promoter'

- After deducting only expenses for printing and stationary, the whole of the proceeds must be devoted to either the provision of prizes or to the purposes of the club, or both

- The only notice or advertisement of the lottery is permitted–

    - On the club premises

    - On the face of the tickets

- The price of every ticket or chance must be the same and if tickets are used the price must be stated on the ticket

- It is illegal to allot free tickets to sellers or to purchasers of complete books of tickets

- The full price of the ticket must be paid on purchase, and no money is returnable to the purchaser

- No ticket in the lottery may be sent through the post

- Prizes in the lottery may be in cash or kind

- 'Printing' includes writing or other modes of reproducing words in visible form; thus, a rubber stamp could be utilised to stamp on the tickets the particulars required by the Act

- Each ticket must have printed on it–

  - The name and address of the promoter

  - To whom it may be sold i.e. members of the club only

  - A statement that no prize will be paid or delivered except to the purchaser of winning tickets

## Society Lotteries

A society is defined as including any club, institution, organisation, association, or persons, by whatever name called, and any separate branch or section of such a club, institution, organisation, or association.

A society lottery means a lottery promoted on behalf of a society which is established and conducted wholly or mainly for one of the following purposes–

- Charitable purposes

- Participation in or support of athletic sports or games, or cultural activities

- Purposes which are not described in the previous two points but are purposes neither of private gain, nor of any commercial undertaking

Society lottery tickets must also state the name and address of the promoter. The proceeds of a society's lottery, after the deduction of amounts for expenses and prizes, must be applied to the purposes of the society.

## Registration Procedure

Once the decision has been taken to promote a lottery, a society must first establish whether it needs to register with its local authority or the Gambling Commission. This will depend on whether the value of tickets that the society i.e. the club intends to put on sale in the lottery will exceed £20,000 or whether, taken together with sales from previous lotteries in the same year, it will exceed £250,000. In either case, such a lottery must be registered with the Gambling Commission. Once it has been decided that commission registration is needed, application forms and further details can be obtained from the commission's lotteries section. No tickets or chances may be offered for sale before the society is registered.

## Frequency and Dates of Lotteries

There are no restrictions on either the number or frequency of lotteries which may be held by a society. The date of a lottery must be specified on the tickets.

## Proceeds Limits

All lotteries promoted by societies under Commission registration are subject to the following limitations–

- The total value of the tickets or chances sold in a single lottery may not exceed £1,000,000

- The total value of the tickets or chances sold in all lotteries held in any one calendar year and promoted on behalf of the same society may not exceed £5,000,000

## Prizes

Prizes in a society lottery may not exceed £25,000 in amount or value, or 10% of the total value of tickets or chances sold, whichever is greater. Not more than 55% of the actual proceeds of a lottery may be used to provide prizes. Where the proceeds of a lottery do not exceed £20,000, up to 35% of the proceeds may be used to meet expenses without referral to the Commission. If the proceeds exceed £20,000, the permitted percentage reduces to 15% but a higher level (up to a maximum of 35%) can be authorised by the Commission in the case of a particular lottery.

## Donated Expenses

In maintaining a record of the expenses of a lottery, it is important that societies take care to ensure that all expenses incurred are included. The records must show whether any expenses were paid by funds other than out of the proceeds of the lottery and, if so, the amount and source of such sums.

## Ticket Requirements

The maximum permitted price of a ticket in a lottery is £1 and the price of every ticket or chance in a lottery must be the same. A person cannot participate in a lottery unless the whole price of the ticket or chance has been paid to the society. In addition, once money has been received for, or on account of, a ticket or chance it cannot be refunded to the participant. No ticket or chance in a lottery may be sold by or to a person under the age of sixteen.

Every ticket must specify–

- Its price
- The name of the society promoting the lottery
- The date of the lottery
- The fact that the society is registered with the Gambling Commission (NB societies promoting lotteries under local authority registration must specify on the ticket the name of the local authority)

### Lottery Returns

After the completion of each lottery promoted under its scheme, the society will be required to submit a lottery return (Form GBL12) to the Commission giving details of the proceeds, expenses and prizes, and showing how the balance of the amount raised was distributed.

### Bingo

Under the Act clubs can offer bingo and other equal chance gaming without a permit or a licence if:

- the club abides by limits in regulations for the amounts which may be deducted from sums staked or won (unless a club gaming permit is held)
- the participation fee is no more than the regulations allow
- games are held on the premises
- games are not linked with games held on other premises
- games are only open to club members and guests (unless your club is a commercial club), and the total stakes or prizes for bingo games played in any seven-day period do not exceed £2,000 more than once in 12 months.

You need to apply for a bingo operating licence if you operate bingo on your club premises with total stakes or prizes that go above £2,000 a week and you plan to do so again at any time during the following 12 months. After the first week of high turnover bingo the club will commit an offence if high turnover bingo is played again in the following 12 months, unless a bingo operating licence has been obtained.

If your total stakes or prizes for bingo reach £2,000 in any seven-day period without an operating licence you must notify the Gambling Commission. Provided conditions outlined in the Act are complied with you do not need a premises licence.

## Under-18s

Persons aged less than 18 years old cannot participate - unless a club admits under-18s to membership and the club does not have a rule against them playing. Bona fide guests less than 18 may also play if club members in the same age group can play.

## Card games

The Commission has developed a code of practice on gaming in clubs. Under certain conditions, clubs are entitled to provide equal chance gaming without a permit or licence. This will include poker with restricted stakes and prizes. If you hold a club gaming permit you will also be permitted to offer

## Other specific games

Clubs do not need an operating licence for card games from the Commission unless there are exceptional circumstances, i.e. the main purpose of the club is gaming. Provided conditions outlined in the Act are complied with you do not need a premises licence.

## Poker, Bridge and Whist

The rules of most clubs provide that no betting shall be permitted on the premises of the club. The term 'betting' is used to describe any game which involves a banker or promoter, whether the bank is a player or the club itself.

Club members are, however, permitted to participate in lawful gaming. The rules of such games must provide that the chances to win are equally favourable to all the players, such as poker, bridge, and whist.

Poker is a card game which, like bridge, involves elements of both chance and skill. It is therefore classified as a game of chance under the Gambling Act 2005. There are many variations on the game of poker. In most forms of the game, players bet or stake progressively into a communal pot and the player holding the best hand at the end of the betting wins the accumulated stakes. Unequal chance poker (e.g. casino stud poker where the banker or dealer participates in the game and holds a mathematical edge over the other players) may only be played in licensed casinos.

Clubs may provide facilities for equal chance card games for their members under the exempt gaming provisions contained in Part 12 of the Gambling Act. There is a stakes limit of £10 per player per game–the limit applies to a game, not a single hand–as well as aggregate stakes limits of £250 per day and £1000 per week for each individual club. For example, a club could run a poker game for twenty-five players paying £10 each four times per week. The maximum prize in a game is £250 and the maximum charge that a club may make for participating in card games is £1 per player per day. No deductions or levies are permitted from either stakes or prizes. Where a club holds a Club Gaming Permit, the maximum participation fee is £3. Where a Club Gaming Permit is held there are no statutory limits on stakes or prizes.

## 6.0 COMMITTEE, OFFICERS AND MEMBERSHIP

### Committee Management

A club is a mutual association of members agreeing to observe certain objects and to provide the social framework most conducive to achieving these objects.

The members may conduct the club's affairs in General Meetings, but it will be obvious that such a method is unwieldy and hardly likely to be efficient. It is more usual to hand over the management to an elected committee of members, who will be responsible for its day-to-day working within the club rules. The management of the club would therefore be vested in the committee.

The rules should specify the number of committee members to be elected. Whilst problems do arise from time to time in finding suitable people who are able and willing to give the necessary time, it is desirable that clubs should have a full complement of officers and committee.

Most clubs are registered under the Licensing Act 2003, enabling them to supply intoxicating liquor. Under that Act, they are required to be managed by one or more 'elective' committees, except where matters are reserved to the club in General Meeting, or for decision by the general body of members.

One of these committees must be the General Management Committee. Where a club is registered under the Friendly Societies Act or the Industrial and Provident Societies Act, the club is regarded as satisfying the requirements to have an elective committee, if that club committee is elected or appointed by its members.

Annual elections must be held for the committee, and the rules should provide how many members shall retire each year.

Each committee member has a personal obligation to see that the club, and its employees, do not break the law. Where committee members deliberately plot or are culpably negligent in failing to prevent a breach of the law, they are personally liable to the penalties provided in law.

All clubs which provide facilities for licensed activities, lawful gaming or lotteries must observe the legislation in respect of them. Apart from this, a committee member's legal liability is small whether a club is registered under the Friendly Societies, Industrial Societies, Companies Acts, or is Unincorporated.

Committee meetings need not be formal affairs if they are conducted in such a way as to secure that business is dealt with as promptly and expeditiously as possible.

It may seem unnecessarily bureaucratic to insist that a committee should have a body of rules for the conduct of its own discussions, but it is preferable to follow set courses of action rather than to let discussions ramble indecisively. Committees can achieve controlled discussions by adopting their own set of Standing Orders. These should cover the power of the Chairman of the committee, voting in committee, the moving and seconding of motions, the order of speaking, and so on.

The right of the Secretary to vote at committee meetings is sometimes disputed, especially where he or she is in receipt of an honorarium. Such a payment does not preclude the Secretary from voting, however. An honorarium is a fee for voluntary service. It does not make the Secretary a paid official. Only where the Secretary is paid under a contract of service should a bar on voting apply. For more details on the question of honoraria, see Chapter 6.0: 'Finance and Accounts.'

Committee motions and amendments should be properly proposed and seconded before they can be discussed, and no motion or amendment should contain a direct negative proposition. The correct procedure in opposing a proposition is for a vote to be cast against it.

Where a vote is tied, the Chairman or whoever is presiding over the committee at the time should have a casting vote and this should be provided for in the Standing Orders. The committee Chairman has an initial vote as a member of the committee and should only use his casting vote where there is a tie. He cannot use this second vote to bring about a tie to defeat a proposition with which he may not agree.

It is important to take votes in the correct order and an amendment must be disposed of before any vote is taken on a substantive motion. There have been examples of this rule being ignored and proceedings reduced to nonsense. In one instance, a motion was carried by six votes to four that a member should not be expelled. But an amendment was then accepted by eight votes to two that he should be expelled. The larger majority was accepted, but if the case had gone to appeal, the member would almost certainly have won. The voting should not have been allowed.

Committee members are not responsible for a club's debts unless they expose themselves to such liability by taking some unauthorised or illegal action. In normal circumstances, they are acting only as agents for the club.

No officer or committee member has an inherent right to draw on the club account. The right to sign cheques may be assigned in the rules or the committee should specify which individuals are authorised to sign cheques on the club's behalf.

## Club Official's Office in Two Clubs

A member of two clubs is not debarred from holding office in one because he holds office in the other. Unless the rules of either club expressly disallow such right, a member of two clubs can claim the privileges of membership of each and the right to hold office in both.

## Duties of Club Officials

Only those prepared to carry out the duties of the club, faithfully and fully, should accept nominations. Elected officers, who include members of the committee, are individually and collectively responsible for ensuring that licensing law and regulations and the club's rules are observed. Their position is one of trust and authority and should be regarded as such. The rules of a club should specify the duties attached to each office.

## The President

He should identify himself actively with the club and its affairs and be more than a figurehead. He should also preside ex officio over all meetings (other than committee meetings).

## The Chairman

Clubs can be very successful when they have a body of enthusiastic and dedicated members, for the membership is the heart of a club and at the head of a club, the Chairman often holds the key to success.

The importance of a hard-working Chairman, together with the Secretary, is paramount. If such a duo also has the support of a hard-working and harmonious committee, then the club will be doubly blessed.

The records of clubs show that many have enjoyed the benefits of devoted Chairmen and Secretaries, without whom the facilities enjoyed by their members would not exist. Therefore, it may be recognised that an important duty of the members is to choose an able and reliable man or woman to represent the club as Chairman.

The Chairman presides ex officio over all committee meetings and, in the absence of the President, those of the club. He should be thoroughly familiar with the rules of the club and the procedures which govern club meetings. He must, always, endeavour to maintain the dignity of his office and, by precept and example, the reputation of the club. The Chairman should not be afraid to exercise his authority, quietly and tactfully, when occasion arises. He should work in the closest co-operation with the Secretary in assuring that all legal and other club obligations are carried out.

Chairmen may be elected directly i.e. by the members in a general meeting or, if the rules provide, indirectly by the committee from among their own number. In the latter case, as the members will have elected all the members of the committee, they will have already signified their confidence in the person who becomes Chairman.

On assuming the responsibilities of the post, the first obligation of a new Chairman is to become familiar with the duties it entails. It would be impossible to describe every situation and problem that might confront a Chairman, which is why the Chairman needs to maintain a cheerful and dignified presence, and to act with tact and fairness always.

The Chairman presides over committee meetings and, consequently, will be instrumental in securing the smooth running of the club and the competent conduct of business. Committee meetings must be held at least once a month to settle club policy, and to make decisions affecting the operations of the club and its development. The Chairman's handling of these meetings will determine, above all, how committee members retain their commitment and interest in serving their club.

The Chairman is the vital link in creating an atmosphere that is indispensable to a successful club. If the Chairman fails, it is possible that one of two trends, or both, will become apparent. There may be a lack of interest among members generally, or difficulties may be experienced in obtaining nominations to fill vacancies occurring on the committee.

Most members learn the art of conducting meetings and running the club and develop the confidence to address a wide audience at general meetings, by working within the committee. An efficient Chairman, who holds the trust of colleagues, will do much to secure the continued success and development of the club. It is up to the Chairman to weld the diverse characters that form a committee into a working unit.

The Chairman will be assisted in his duties if there is a code of standing orders which the committee members themselves have accepted and agreed upon for the proper conduct of their affairs. In conjunction with the Secretary, the Chairman is responsible for arranging the agenda and the priorities of the committee. A carefully prepared agenda will help to ensure that business may be dealt with quickly. If all essential business is catered for and all correspondence considered, their choice of priorities is unlikely to cause dissention within the committee.

If an agenda cannot be completed in time, it is better that the committee should agree to adjourn to a later date to conclude the outstanding business. The Chairman and Secretary should not take it upon themselves to omit items from the agenda to shorten the meeting. It is for the committee to decide what they will consider for the business is theirs and needs to be dealt with. The authority of the committee should never be usurped. However, a good Chairman will be able to influence them towards wise decisions.

Patience and the avoidance of argument are the best instruments for the smooth conduct of meetings. It should go without saying that the Chairman must conduct meetings in accordance with club rules, standing orders and recognised rules of procedure. This may not guarantee totally trouble-free meetings in all circumstances, but it will prevent most problems from occurring. If the occasion does occur when disorderliness develops, and the Chairman believes business cannot be satisfactorily concluded, the meeting may be adjourned to another date.

In addition, a Chairman should remember that a committee never performs the tasks which are specifically allotted to individual officers or the steward. Not only is this likely to be both confusing and a waste of the committee's time, it can be irritating and frustrating for an intelligent body of people who have given their time to committee work to find they are also engaged in trying to perform duties specifically allocated elsewhere. Similarly, neither the officers nor employees should be allowed to take decisions that are the prerogative of the committee collectively.

The Chairman will fulfil the duties of chairmanship by adopting a conciliatory attitude and try to avoid riding roughshod over even the most awkward participant from the floor. A cheerful, firm, tactful and judicious person will avoid most of the possible pitfalls of chairmanship and earn grateful thanks from the membership.

## Trustees

The dictionary definition of the word 'trustee' sums up what is expected of such an office holder. The definition says, simply, 'one who is trusted or to whom something is entrusted.' It adds that the definition in law is 'one to whom property is entrusted for the benefit of another; one of a number of persons appointed to manage the affairs of an institution.' Even on that basis it is clearly not a task that should be undertaken lightly. It is not an office held just for the honour itself, although many justifiably regard it as an honour bestowed by the club.

Trustees must be eighteen years of age or over and elected by members of the club at a General Meeting. They are usually ex officio members of the club committee by virtue of their office. Trustees attend meetings and are subject to the decisions of the committee. Neither the Secretary nor Treasurer of a club should hold the office of trustee.

Trustees are appointed 'at the pleasure of the club' which, in ordinary language, means until resignation, removal or death. It is possible for the club rules to provide for a fixed term of years. Rules should state the method of election or appointment of trustees and how the tenure of office is terminable subject to any separate deeds. On the election of a new trustee, a Deed of Appointment must always be made, and conveyances updated. The committee must see to it that the club's lawyers are involved in the appointment of the elected trustee to his office so that the essential legal formalities are carried out. The lawyers, too, must be involved when a trustee is 'discharged' at the end of his or her term, or when death, in office, occurs.

It is very important that club trustees gain an understanding of their position. It is essential for trustees to appreciate fully, what they are called upon to do, what they do and why they are doing it so that they do not, through inadvertence, become personally liable. They must always remember that they are acting on behalf of the club.

Legal proceedings are taken in the name of the trustees on behalf of or against the club unless its rules specify some other person. Orders obtained against trustees do not lie against the property and possessions owned personally by the trustees but against the assets of the club. This is the case providing they are suitably indemnified, which should be in the club's rules, and they have been appointed properly by Deed of Appointment. In other words, trustees' personal effects are not at risk if they are involved in legal proceedings on behalf of the club so long as they have acted strictly within the club rules. If they have knowingly allowed the club funds to be used for objects not authorised by the rules, they become personally liable.

All leases and agreements of the club should be in the names of the trustees and no documents should be signed by them until they are satisfied, they are acting on behalf of the club. Clubs must seek advice when any documents are to be signed that involve the future of the club, its property, or its finances no matter who is the other party involved. It is vital that such documents and anything similar should be examined and approved by the club's legal advisers before signature. The club might well have to pay a fee for expert advice, but the peace of mind which it can bring will be well worth the expenditure.

Trustees must pay attention to the use of club funds and must always ensure that no moneys of the club are spent contrary to law or the club rules, or for purposes not connected with the club or its objects. Proceedings against any person or persons, for fraud or misappropriation, are instituted in the names of the trustees. Two of the duties of trustees which are generally well known are that they are the people, when things have gone badly wrong, who sue on behalf of the club and those who are sued as representatives of the club.

For generations in the club movement, the appointment to the position of trustee has been perceived as the very peak of achievement. Trustees are chosen from members who have served their club well and faithfully and sometimes the appointment is seen as a 'reward' for their fidelity and long service. That however must not be the sole consideration.

Anyone being considered for the position of trustee must be a person of integrity, held in high regard and be ready to play a full part in the life of the club. Older members will bring the benefit of a lifetime of experience in the club and the outside world to the office. However, the case for the appointment of a younger person who can build up the knowledge required while working alongside an older trustee should not be dismissed. Whatever the age of the trustee, clubs should bear in mind, and have faith in, his or her judgement, integrity, and continuing devotion to the interests of club members. At all times trustees must ensure that whatever they do is in strict accordance with the rules of the club and with law and regulations.

Another very important point is to ensure that a club is never left with only one trustee. The number of trustees set out in the club's rules should always be maintained. This is necessary because if the one remaining trustee dies, then the 'statutory vesting' of the club's property passes to his executors or administrators. It is important to remember this procedure, as failure to follow it could lead to difficulties which, in turn, could lead to a costly legal process to resolve.

If the need arises to remove a trustee from office, a Special General Meeting should be summoned in the manner laid down in the club rules. The rules should also state by what majority such action can be taken. Remember, a vacancy created in this way must be filled–and the appointment made in the correct manner–without delay.

## The Treasurer

The Treasurer is responsible for seeing that all moneys, whether received by himself, the Secretary, the steward or any other official or employee are duly banked. He is to ensure that all debts of the club are paid as directed by the committee and that cheques are signed by himself and one, or more, members of the Finance Committee, then countersigned by the Secretary. It is his duty to produce the Paying-in Book, Bank Statement, Daily Takings Book etc. at every meeting of the committee, or whenever required.

## The Secretary

It is the duty of the Secretary to keep the books, documents, and papers of the club in proper order and carefully filed. He must summon and attend all meetings and take Minutes of the proceedings. Other responsibilities may be summarised–

- Keep the register of members up to date, with record of last payment of subscriptions

- See that the names, addresses and occupations of candidates for membership are duly displayed on the club notice board for the period stipulated in the rules

- Issue notices of default to members in arrears and see that names are removed from the register if subscriptions are not paid within the period stated in the rules

- Post all notices in connection with General or Special General Meetings

- Check nominations of candidates for office and allow none to go forward which are not in order

- Comply with the requirements of the Licensing Act 2003

- Comply with the requirements of the National Insurance Acts, Statutory Sick Pay and see that all paid employees are insured

- See that the club is insured against liability at Common Law, for accidents occurring to club employees, and against fire and burglary

The duties imposed on a club's Secretary make the person undertaking this office the linchpin in the conduct of club affairs. Unless the Secretary is truly competent, a club will find that it is unable to operate effectively and in accordance with the increasingly complex legislation affecting clubs. The Secretary acts under the superintendence, control, and direction of the committee of management and is responsible for seeing that the decisions of the committee are conveyed to the proper quarter.

The position of Secretary requires not only considerable administrative skills but must also fulfil the vital role of providing liaison between the membership and the committee. The Secretary's basic functions are to ensure that the club's clerical and organising activities are carried out, to see that all subscriptions are collected, and that correspondence is dealt with.

A competent Secretary should be thoroughly familiar with the rules of his club, so that he can advise authoritatively when necessary. He should possess an intimate knowledge of the Licensing Act in so far as it applies to clubs. He is the official primarily held responsible in law for seeing that its provisions are complied with. The Secretary might be made a party to any proceedings instigated against the club for any breach of the requirements of the Licensing Act. Therefore, the Secretary must be conversant with the demands of licensing and gaming laws and of registration and other statutory duties under the Licensing, Friendly Societies, and Industrial and Provident Societies Acts. Failure to meet some of these requirements will cause the Secretary to be held personally liable. A plea that it was committed without his knowledge and connivance would be a good defence to any proceedings taken against him personally, if it could be established.

Before considering the possibilities surrounding the choice of Secretary, it must be reiterated that the Secretary, like the Chairman, requires qualities of integrity and impartiality and must be capable of commanding the respect of members. He should be a good mixer who does not yield to the influences of pressure groups or factions within the club and is not suspected of favouritism. Again, he must always be aware that he is responsible to the committee and the members for his actions, and that his decisions must reflect the policies of the committee.

The choice of Secretary is governed by the rules and the period of tenure is determined by them. They should be sufficiently flexible to enable members either to elect or to appoint a Secretary, depending on their view of the post's requirements. Rules should include a provision for clubs to choose between electing a member from their own ranks, or to appoint some other person. Among the many reasons for members preferring an elected Secretary is that they may feel it possible for him to cope with the work entailed on a part-time basis. Certainly, the volume of work falling to the Secretary will be a fundamental pointer in deciding whether the post should be filled by election or appointment.

If the club chooses to elect a secretary, then the election takes place in the same way as for any other officer. If elected, the Secretary remains a member of the club. He will be entitled to propose or second motions, and to speak and vote both in committee and in General Meetings just like any other officer or club member.

Larger clubs may consider that the demands placed on their Secretary are beyond the capacity of a voluntary officer. The appointment of a Secretary is not normally made by members in general. The committee makes such appointments just as they appoint other employees of the club. Applicants may come from within the membership or from outside. Therefore, the rules customarily provide that where an appointed Secretary is to be preferred, the committee will carry out the appointment. In this position he is an officer without power, except as delegated by the committee.

## Committee

It is the duty of the committee to attend their meetings regularly. The committee conduct the general business of the club; are responsible for its management and control, and for seeing that the rules are duly observed. Acting in a quasi-judicial capacity they are empowered–subject to what the rules say–to suspend or expel offending members, having first given them an opportunity of being heard in self-defence. The appointment, control and dismissal of all club employees rest solely in the hands of the committee.

The committee is responsible for checking books kept by the Treasurer or Secretary and seeing that all takings have been duly paid into the bank. They should examine the Order Book and be satisfied that only goods authorised by them have been purchased and that accounts submitted for payment have been duly checked and verified with the Goods Received Book kept by the Steward. The committee, realising their position of trust and authority, should rigidly observe the rules of the club, thus setting an example to the members.

## Election of Club Officials

The rules of a club should provide the method whereby its officers and committee are elected. Such rules must be strictly adhered to, otherwise the election may be rendered invalid and a fresh ballot must be taken. What follows should be read and applied subject to anything appearing to the contrary in the club rules.

## Nominations

It is the duty of Secretary to post a nomination sheet on the notice board, which records the names of candidates for the committee or other offices. The nomination sheet must remain displayed for whole period stipulated in club's rules. Day and time when nominations close should be stated on the sheet, even if not definitely fixed by club rules. The proposer and the seconder of any candidate should personally sign their names against the candidate they put forward, having previously ascertained that their nominee is willing to stand and serve if elected. A member may be nominated for any number of offices in the club unless the rules provide otherwise; if elected to more than one office, he can select the one he desires to hold. If the rules say that no candidate shall be nominated for more than one office, it is permitted for an officer or committee member who is not due to retire to be nominated for another office without first resigning. If unsuccessful, he would retain his present office.

## Qualifications

Candidates for office, nominators and seconders must be either honorary members, life members, or subscribing members who are not in arrears with payment of their subscription before nomination sheet is due to be taken down. Otherwise nominations may be objected. Where a rule provides that a certain period of membership is an essential qualification for office, this must be calculated from the date when the candidate was elected to membership to the last day of nominations. For example, should six months be specified, a person elected to membership on 6 July would first become eligible on 6 January the following year.

## List of Voters

Unless the rules provide otherwise, every member of the club is entitled to vote. It is the duty of the Secretary to prepare a special list of members for this purpose. The list should be handed to scrutineers, together with the precise number of requisite ballot papers if all such members voted.

## Ballot Paper

The ballot paper is compiled from the nomination sheet. In preparing the ballot paper, names of candidates for presidency and other offices are usually typed or printed in separate sections on the same sheet as names of candidates for committee. The different sections are nevertheless distinct, and if one section is spoilt by the voter, it does not invalidate other sections.

Names of all candidates should be set out alphabetically on the ballot paper and in uniform type. The 'starring' of ballot papers i.e. putting an asterisk (*) against the names of retiring members seeking re-election or distinguishing them by printing their names in larger or thicker type is irregular.

## Marking the Ballot Paper

If a voter makes some mark other than the customary 'X' against the name of the candidate for whom he wishes to vote, it does not necessarily spoil his paper. The vote is good if the intention of the voter is clear. Practically the only grounds for the rejection of the paper are–

- Because too many votes have been recorded

- Uncertainty of the voter's intention

- Writing enough to identify the voter

If a member spoils a paper he should, on request, be supplied with another, having previously handed back the one spoilt. A member may vote for a fewer number of candidates than there are vacancies–he cannot be compelled to use all his votes–but if he votes for more candidates than there are vacancies, the paper, so far as the particular section is concerned, must be regarded as spoilt.

## Taking the Ballot

Unless the rules contain specific instructions on the matter, committees decide how ballot papers are to be distributed – whether sent to members by post or handed to them on request. Where the former method is adopted and the member returns the paper by post or hand, the envelope containing it should be sealed and marked 'ballot.' It should be addressed to the scrutineers, who must deposit it unopened in the ballot box. Where ballot papers are handed to members, the scrutineers should first make sure from the list received from the Secretary that the member is entitled to vote. When this is done, the member's name should be scored off, thus preventing anyone voting twice.

## Close of Ballot

The ballot must remain open the full time stated in the rules. When it is closed, the scrutineers count the votes recorded. The results, signed by them, together with the marked list of members to whom they have handed ballot papers, and all unused ballot papers, must be handed by them to the Chairman at the Annual General Meeting.

## Demand for a Scrutiny

If a majority of the meeting demands a scrutiny, the box containing all the ballot papers should be sealed by the Chairman and arrangements made for a recount in the presence of the scrutineers. Once it has been declared and accepted, a ballot stands no matter what discrepancies a subsequent examination of the papers may reveal. Prior to the signed statement being handed to the Chairman by the scrutineers, a system of checking and double checking should be carried out to ensure absolute accuracy in the matter of the votes recorded.

## The Important Role of Sub-Committees

Sub-committees are the last level of management of a club. Clubs are required under the Licensing Act to have one general management committee, but they may have more committees. For larger clubs, these extra committees are essential, and for smaller clubs they can be extremely valuable.

The rules do not have to specify which sub-committees shall be appointed. It is usually enough for the general committee to be given the power to appoint such sub-committees as they deem necessary to assist them in their overall task of managing the club's affairs. Two sub-committees generally set up by clubs are a Finance sub-committee and a Bar sub-committee. Others may include an Entertainment sub-committee and a Games sub-committee.

Sub-committees are either appointed or elected and they perform specific and specialised tasks. Their membership does not have to be composed entirely of persons elected from the club committee. However, any member of a sub-committee who is a member of the general committee would be required to stand down from the sub-committee if they resign from the general committee. Also, any sub-committee concerned with the purchase or supply of intoxicating liquor on the club's behalf, must consist of members duly elected by the club membership.

There are numerous opportunities in a club for the use of sub-committees where appointment and co-option may be used to employ the services of a wide range of members. Sub-committees provide the opportunity to bring in all the best talent available to make the conduct of affairs successful and improve the events and amenities of the club. A member who is an accountant may plead that he does not have the time to participate in all the functions of the general committee, though he can be an invaluable member of a Finance sub-committee. Members with experience in leisure industries will be attractive as recruits to an Entertainment sub-committee. Co-option to sub-committees also provides the chance for younger club members to learn management procedure.

Sub-committees can elect their own officers and adopt their own procedures however ultimately, they are always responsible to the general committee. They are not usually entitled to make decisions affecting the club without the approval of the general committee. This is especially true where the sub-committee makes proposals involving the use of club funds. For example, the Entertainment or Social sub-committee could be charged with running the annual dinner or a monthly dance. As such it should either obtain an estimate cost for approval by the general committee, or that committee must specify a maximum sum within which the sub-committee plans its expenditure. If the sub-committee finds it cannot contain spending within the limit laid down, it must report back to the general committee giving its reasons and asking for the limit to be raised.

The mechanics may not be the same in each club but the principle to be observed is that sub-committees must have the approval of the general committee for what they wish to do. There is a danger that members of sub-committees will believe they have a special remit of the authority of the general committee. This view must be resisted. Serious financial consequences might follow if the general committee does not have the last word in managing the club within the powers given them by the rules.

Nevertheless, members of sub-committees are not puppets. It might be difficult to find people to serve on them if they were asked to regard themselves in this way. All who serve on sub-committees should be aware not only of their powers, but also where the boundaries of those powers fall.

Sub-committees are of tremendous importance to the well-being of the club. If they are to function well, sub-committee members should be familiar with the requirements of the club's rules and the laws relating to the conduct of Private Members' Clubs, just as much as the officers and general committee. An Entertainment sub-committee, for instance, must be conversant with the conditions applicable to the promotion of bingo and lotteries, and to the limitations on serving drink at social functions.

### Disciplinary Procedure: Suspension and Expulsion

There are occasionally people whose actions cause offence and/or discomfort to others, and there are some whose conduct will be such that action has to be taken. Such action can appear distasteful, complex, and difficult but club officers and committees must realise that some of the jobs they undertake are not easy.

It is essential to carry out this difficult task to ensure that the other members can enjoy the comfort and benefits of a well conducted club. It is right that before such proceedings are commenced club officers must be guided by what is best for the club and for other members.

For the purpose of inquiring into the conduct of a member, it is desirable to summon a special meeting of the committee or, at any rate, exercise great care to ensure that every member of it is definitely informed that the case is to be considered, so that all who desire to be present are afforded an opportunity of attending. When the conduct of more than one member is to be investigated in connection with the same incident, it is within the sole discretion of the committee how the inquiry shall be conducted, whether those summoned shall appear before them singly or together.

Anyone involved in disciplinary proceedings must follow, to the absolute letter, the correct procedure. The golden rule which must always be remembered is 'consult the club's own authorised rule book.' It is essential that all club officers should have a basic understanding of what can and cannot be done when they are faced with the unpleasant task of dealing with a member whose behaviour has fallen well below what is expected in a club.

It is my hope that your committee will not have to resort to calling a meeting to discuss 'disciplinary action' but there are times when there is no alternative and acting becomes a necessity. At all stages, the alleged offender must be treated judicially and with a proper regard for natural justice.

In any disciplinary proceedings it is essential that the member complained about must be given full details of the complaint made against him. Also, he must be given the opportunity to: answer the complaints in person; hear the evidence against him from other persons; ask questions of those persons before the committee; and call his own witnesses.

If a member's behaviour inside the club is contrary to the rules, then most rules provide that either the Chairman or Secretary has the authority to order the member's withdrawal. Such a member cannot be excluded indefinitely. Any automatic withdrawal should be reported to the committee as soon as possible. Most club rules provide that a committee meeting should be held within seven days of the alleged offence.

When the committee consider the complaint, they may decide that no further action is required. In such cases, the member is free to resume his membership facilities and should always be advised of this decision as soon as possible. However, if the committee decide that the initial withdrawal requires further investigation then a disciplinary hearing date should be fixed and the member in question notified that the facilities of his membership remain withdrawn until he is summoned to appear before the committee.

In any other case of misconduct, for example when a written complaint is made to the Secretary concerning a member's behaviour, the complaint should be dealt with at the next regular committee meeting. Again, if the committee consider that no further action is necessary, the complainant should be informed. If, however, the committee does warrant further investigation, the member in question should be informed that the facilities of membership are withdrawn until a disciplinary hearing is convened.

The offending member should be summoned, in writing, to appear before the committee. The notice must include the date and time of the meeting and a statement setting out full details of the complaint. It is not enough to simply ask the member to 'explain his conduct.' If a specific statement is not included with the summons to appear before the committee, there could be grounds for appeal against any disciplinary decision, since the member is unable to prepare a defence. The summons should be sent by registered post. Usually, a week's notice is given. At the meeting he should be heard in self-defence and allowed to call witnesses should he desire to do so.

A committee is acting as a quasi-judicial body when it holds a disciplinary hearing and consequently the committee may not hand out a decision summarily without listening to any statement the accused member wishes to make or any witness he wishes to call. One is not expected to appear in court without being made fully aware of the allegations being made.

When a member appears before a committee, the following procedure is suggested—

- The Secretary reads out details of the member's alleged offence

- Whoever is charged with conducting the case of the club gives the facts and indicates clearly the rules alleged to have been broken i.e. the grounds for the case

- Where witnesses are to be called, for the club or by the defending member, they remain outside the room until required to give their evidence; after then, they remain in the room

- The member remains in the room throughout the hearing; he must be allowed to cross-examine the club's witnesses

- When these witnesses have been heard, the member makes his own statement and calls his own witnesses to speak in his defence.; both he and the committee may put questions to the witnesses

- After all the evidence has been heard, it is usual, but not essential, for the person presenting the club's case to sum up and to make any additional comments on the evidence given

- Similarly, the member accused must be allowed to make any further statement he wishes, and this concludes the presentation of the case

- Then the committee retires to consider their decision; alternatively, the member and all the witnesses withdraw while they do so

Should the member (or members) whose conduct is in question fail to appear before the committee at the stipulated time, or afford a bona fide excuse for non-attendance, he can either be written to again and summoned to attend the next meeting, or the case can be dealt with in his absence. Every reasonable opportunity should be given to the member to attend and answer the charge against him.

If the committee does not think it is enough to deal with any case by a reprimand, then most club rules provide for two-thirds of those present to vote for suspension or expulsion.

Suspension must be for a definite period and the date when it expires recorded in the minutes. For a member to be suspended 'until he appears before the committee' is improper. The suspension should not exceed one year. It is not open to the committee to suspend a member sine die, which means 'with no date fixed.' For the period of suspension, a member is denied entry to the club premises and the enjoyment of its privileges. Nor should he be admitted to another club as an affiliated member.

A member is liable to pay subscriptions, even if under suspension. He has no right to the return of any subscription paid in advance should he be expelled or resign. If the subscription is increased in accordance with the rules, he is liable for the altered rate agreed upon, if the rules so provide. Any suspended member who has not paid when the time for paying subscriptions has elapsed will cease to be a member. A member under suspension remains liable for his subscription but forfeits all privileges of membership while the suspension is in operation.

Should a committee member commit an offence then disciplinary treatment must be imposed in the same way as any other club member. If a member of the committee is suspended, they are unable to attend meetings of the committee. Most club rules provide that a member of the committee who is suspended automatically vacates his seat as his absence does not constitute a 'reasonable excuse' for nonattendance. Accordingly, if he has been absent the stipulated number of times under the rule governing such matters, he vacates his seat. If accused though, a committee member has no right to be present when the remainder of the committee are considering the case.

Expulsion is a more serious affair. A person's reputation is at stake and, if expelled, he will suffer in the eyes of fellow members, and possibly the wider community. Again, close attention must be paid to the club's rule book. Committees occasionally make up their minds before the hearing, and consequently tend to overlook proceedings.

When voting, after the member has given his version and withdrawn, the proposal to expel him must be put 'for' or 'against.' If an amendment is moved–say, that instead of being expelled he shall be suspended for a period– the amendment must first be voted on. If this is defeated, the resolution to expel must then be put. Once a member's case has been considered by the committee and the required majority of votes for expulsion or suspension have not been obtained, the matter is at an end and cannot be re-opened at any subsequent meeting.

Names of members suspended or expelled should not be posted in the club; it is enough to inform the steward and doorkeeper. All correspondence relating to expulsions and suspensions should be carefully filed, including the letter conveying the decision of the committee.

Most rules state that a committee's decision in all disciplinary matters is final, and therefore a disciplined member would have no right to seek a Special General Meeting to appeal to the general membership against a decision. Some rules, however, include an appeal rule which provides arbitration facilities to aggrieved members.

Such rules differ from club to club and the extent to which appeal rules apply will often depend on how the club is registered. For example, a club which is incorporated under the Industrial and Provident Societies Acts is obliged to include a disputes rule. However, such a rule cannot deal with an appeal against expulsion because this subject has been excluded from the statutes.

If an aggrieved member is unable to apply for arbitration under the rules, then he may seek the guidance of a solicitor and, if so advised, take proceedings against the club through the courts. A court will not interfere with the findings of a 'domestic tribunal' if it considers the tribunal, or in the case of clubs the committee, has acted fairly and in accordance with its own rules. That confidence is most likely to be justified if the committee have paid full attention to their rules, and followed the procedures outlined above.

Should a member be convicted in a court of law of an offence which, in the opinion of the committee, is of such a nature to render him unfit for continued membership of the club, he can be expelled, without being summoned before the committee, but only if it is specifically so stated in the club's rules.

However, a member may well have made a plea in mitigation before the court with which the court had great sympathy and of which the committee may be totally unaware. The member should invariably therefore be given the opportunity of appearing before the committee to make any plea in mitigation of the offence he wishes, or alternatively to submit these in writing to the committee. In all other cases, a normal disciplinary hearing should be held. This is considered desirable even if the club's rules provide otherwise.

In summary therefore, a member cannot be expelled or suspended, unless he has been informed of the charge against him and given due opportunity of being heard in self-defence by being summoned to appear before the committee. The rules governing suspension and expulsion must be carried out to the letter; then if the decision arrived at is bona fide (without malice) no court will be able to interfere with it.

## Discipline and Misconduct Flowchart

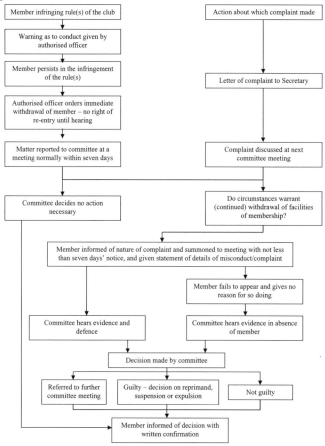

This flow chart is for explanatory purposes only and is not a substitute for the rules. For all formal purposes, the rules should be consulted.

## Membership Recruitment

Apart from financial control, the key to a club's future success lies in the ability to recruit new members. In most clubs, whatever facilities are available, only one third of the total membership uses the club regularly and its hard core is less than this. The aim, therefore, is to increase the total membership to increase the proportion which makes up one third.

Membership recruitment is a matter which should be discussed regularly by committees. Without a continuous programme of membership recruitment, a club will eventually weaken. Club committees often place the onus of responsibility for recruiting new members on themselves, rather than correctly placing it on the membership. It is the members who must propose and second new members, not just the committee.

It does seem that people are often encouraged to become involved in membership recruitment if there is some form of reward involved. One of the most successful recruitment schemes is known as the 'bounty system,' whereby a member who introduces a new member receives some form of payment, usually by way of a bar voucher. For example, if a club's membership subscription is £10, the payment of a £10 bar voucher to the introductory member (which will actually only cost the club the value of the stock, rather than the whole £10) has in many cases created a great deal of interest.

A further method, which has often proved successful, is the announcement that the club intends to close the membership book. You would be surprised how many people will suddenly wish to become members of a club if they think the club will be difficult to join. I suspect that human nature dictates that most of us wish to belong to something which has an element of exclusivity.

Experience has also shown that many clubs will recruit new members and will lose them at the following year's renewal time. I believe one of the reasons for this is that new members are not always made as welcome as they should be. All clubs, by their very nature, tend to have established groups and sections and these can seem daunting to a new person using the club for the first time. Three or four new members' evenings should be organised during the year to which all members who have joined during the previous period are invited. These social occasions are a great way to help 'break the ice' and forge friendships with existing members.

## Club Advertising

Care must be taken not to advertise directly for new members. Club rules should contain a reference to candidates for membership being properly proposed and seconded by existing members who are able to vouch for their suitability. This is one of the fundamental principles which define a bona fide members' club, as opposed to a club which allows people to come in and drink following some mere administrative 'tick the box'.

Licensing Authorities grant a club a Club Premises Certificate (CPC) on the grounds that they are managed in accordance with their rules, and that the rules comply with the Licensing Act 2003. Committees will appreciate therefore that, by advertising directly for new members, a club would effectively be announcing the fact that it is not complying with its own rules.

It is possible to place an advertisement in the local press or on a flyer posted to local residential or business addresses, which for example, lists forthcoming events and facilities which are on offer, provided the following words are included–

*'Members, Members' Guests and Affiliation Ticket holders welcome. For further details please contact the Secretary.'*

It is likely that non-members will read this advertisement and may be attracted to what is happening at the club and the facilities which are on offer and may indeed contact the club with a view to becoming members. Importantly, however, the club could not be accused of advertising for members. Some clubs have successfully used this method to highlight the club and its activities with the result of increased patronage by existing members who are able to see what activities are planned as well as interest from non-members who may wish to become members of the club.


## Audit Requirements

Clubs registered under the Industrial and Provident Societies Acts or under the Friendly Societies Act must have their accounts audited annually. The professional audit thresholds for non-deposit taking societies under the 1965 and 1974 Acts have been amended to bring them closer into line with those of companies, so that many more societies are not required to have a professional audit. Rules for Industrial and Provident Societies should provide clubs with the option of taking advantage of the new relaxation in audit requirements, but also provide that members can vote to request a full audit in any one year.

The following table sets out the financial parameters which determine the type of audit required by clubs registered under the Industrial and Provident Societies Acts–

| Audit Type | Criteria |
| --- | --- |
| Full Audit | Previous year's turnover exceeds £5,600,000 (£250,00 if charitable), or total assets exceeded £2,800,000 |
| Lay Audit | The total of the society's receipts and payments (income and expenditure) in the previous year did not exceed £5,000, and the total number of members at the yearend did not exceed 500 and the total assets did not exceed £5,000 |
| Accountant's Report | Previous year's turnover exceeds £90,000 but does not exceed £5,600,000 (£250,00 if charitable), and total assets do not exceed £2,800,000 |
| Un-audited | Previous year's turnover did not exceed £90,000, and total assets did not exceed £2,800,000 |

Clubs registered under the Industrial and Provident Societies Act or the Friendly Societies Acts must submit an annual return to the Financial Conduct Authority no later than the date required under the terms of the club's rules. Failure to comply may result in prosecution. Such clubs must also ensure the annual fee is paid, the amount of which depends upon the club's assets.

Clubs which are incorporated as companies must ensure that their company returns are made to Companies House by the agreed submission date to avoid fines and that their accounts are filed.

Unincorporated members' clubs are not required to submit annual returns or to file accounts with any outside body. The audit requirements of such clubs are only those which are set out in a club's individual rules. However, Section 63 of the Licensing Act 2003 requires that–

- All clubs have arrangements in place for giving information to members about the finances of the club

- Books of accounts and other records are kept ensuring the accuracy of that information

## Corporation Tax

Members' clubs are regarded as Mutual Trading Associations by HMRC, where the transactions are confined solely to members. Therefore, clubs are not liable for corporation tax on any surplus. If, however a club derives any income from bank deposits, investments, property, or occupation of land, it is liable for corporation tax. HMRC can assess and claim any corporation tax within six years after the expiration of the year of assessment for which the club should have been charged or more in certain cases. On request, a club must send a copy of its balance sheet to the Inspector of Taxes.

## VAT and Room Hire

Exemption of VAT on room hire is rarely volunteered by HMRC. However, below is an extract from VAT Notice 701/5 which may be of interest to many clubs, club accountants and auditors–

'*10. Hire of Rooms and Halls*

*10.1 What is the VAT liability of my supply of the hire of rooms and halls?*

*The hire of a room or hall is exempt from VAT provided that–*

- *the person to whom you are hiring the room or hall has exclusive occupation of it during the period of hire*

- *the room or hall is not designed or equipped for sport or physical recreation, which excludes such places as gyms and sports halls*

- *you have not 'opted to tax' the building in which the room or hall is situated.*

*10.2 What is included in the exemption?*

*This exemption includes–*

- *facilities such as a kitchen or bar area within the room or next to it*

- *those fixtures and fittings that form a part of the hire, for example lighting and sound equipment if the room is used as a discotheque.'*

## Honoraria

An honorarium is not a salary; it is a 'voluntary fee for a voluntary service.' HMRC defines honoraria as payment made to officeholders for doing something they are not rewarded for in any other way. Either the members in general meeting or the committee may grant such persons an honorarium in recognition of those services, provided the rules permit.

Many clubs assume that, because they are often of insignificant amounts, honoraria are tax-free. This is not the case. Payments of honoraria, whatever the amount, are subject to Income Tax and National Insurance and must be included and dealt with in accordance with the rules of PAYE in the same way as the payment of wages or salaries to club employees.

Straightforward payment or reimbursement of out-of-pocket expenses will not normally attract Income Tax. However, honoraria, which are not specifically linked to recognisable expenditure, are taxable. HMRC Inspectors have the authority to backdate unpaid tax six years. In one case, this liability amounted to a staggering £40,000.

If your club is paying honoraria for the first time, or if payments made in the past have not been taxed under PAYE, then your Tax Office will advise you what to do. Your correct Tax Office is the one dealing with the club, not the Tax Office of the person in receipt of the honorarium.

## Club Wins Important Case at Employment Tribunal: Unfair Dismissal Claim Rejected

The rather unusual circumstances of this case began when an officer of the club resigned from their position following the committee's decision to reduce the allocation of honorarium for the officer's position. This person then brought a claim of 'unfair dismissal' arguing that the club was in fundamental breach of contract by reducing the payment.

In order to succeed in a claim for unfair dismissal however, it was necessary to establish that this person was an employee of the club, and it is this specific issue–the definition of an honorarium in an employment context–which made this case so important. When the case was originally heard, the Employment Tribunal decided that the applicant's case be dismissed. The Tribunal determined that the officer was not an employee of the club.

The former officer lodged an appeal and the Appeal Tribunal stated that the first hearing might have failed to properly analyse the actual status of the applicant in relation all the factors relevant to the position held. The Appeal Tribunal requested that a fresh hearing be held.

The unanimous decision of the second Employment Tribunal was to dismiss the application because the former officer was not a club employee and therefore had no employment rights.

The conclusion of the Employment Tribunal was as follows–

*The Employment Appeal Tribunal identified this case as being one of potential importance to clubs.*

*We consider the applicant's voluntary undertaking to be no more and no less than that which many people volunteer to undertake to assist in the running of clubs and societies to which they may belong.*

*The Tribunal does not consider the characteristics of the applicant's relationship with the respondent to be one of master and servant, or employer and employee.*

*The relationship cannot be properly characterised as constituting an employment contract given all the circumstances which we have identified and therefore the applicant's claim must be dismissed.'*

The importance of this unprecedented case, to establish that the payment of honoraria does not constitute employed status, is significant.

## Financial Controls

All clubs must rely on the honesty and integrity of their elected officers and committee members. However, betrayal of trust can take many forms – taking a bottle or two out of stock, the odd free drink, or some loose change, or several thousand pounds from the club's funds.

Fortunately, such thefts are not a regular occurrence, but every committee must be aware that such unhappy incidents can, and do, take place. Club funds provide the lifeblood of the club and its activities and theft is not a crime without a victim. All members of the club are victims of such a crime, and it is not a matter that can just be wished away or ignored.

For many years, it has been recommended that every club should have fidelity insurance within its insurance policy. Obviously, this will involve extra expense for the club, but it is money well spent to ensure that the club is protected against the defaults of a trusted officer or employee. Such insurance should cover all the club officers and stewards who handle cash at some time in the course of their duties. This is in addition to the steward's bond.

There is no doubt that even suggesting the possibility of fidelity insurance at a committee meeting will cause a great deal of embarrassment that serving officers and employees are being accused of dishonesty. Such embarrassment is misplaced, however. Committees should act in the best interests of the club and it is no insult to suggest that the names of certain officers be added to the insurance. It is no slight on their character. It does not mean there are any suspicions or that rumours are circulating about their honesty.

## Financial Controls Checklist

- One club officer should be present each day with the steward to check the takings from the till(s); this will provide an independent check of cash takings against till readings
- Tills should be serviced regularly and there should be strict control of till roll issues and usage; any till that is reported out of order frequently should be treated with suspicion and investigated

- All completed till rolls should be returned to the Treasurer
- Takings should be banked daily, and two people should take the money to the bank; for the security of those involved, times and routes taken should vary
- The Treasurer should produce the latest bank statements at each committee meeting and the committee must never be put off by any excuse for the statements not being produced
- Blank cheques should never be signed – this seems an obvious safeguard, but it can be overlooked
- If books are said to be 'with the auditors,' the Chairman or Secretary should confirm that this is so
- The Secretary or another committee member should always be present at stocktaking
- Ideally, there should be no more than two keys to the bar or cellar stocks – one should be held by the steward and another by the Secretary or a designated committee member who must never lend it out
- If stocktaking reveals stock shortages, there must be an immediate investigation
- Independent stock checks should be made on deliveries from time to time and irregularly
- Do not forget the importance of fidelity insurance and to comply with the requirements imposed by the insurance policy

It is vital that no one person is left to handle everything however willing he or she may be to take on such an onerous burden. Clubs will benefit from shared responsibilities and double checks.

## Gaming Machine Finance

A club's gaming machines are, without doubt, the most common area of concern in respect of thefts. It is essential that a proper, recognised system of emptying the gaming machines is established not only to protect the club but also to protect the committee from malicious accusations of theft.

The following procedure is recommended to clubs:

- The keys to gaming machines should not be held by one person or should be only accessible from a double-locked key safe where the keys are held by more than one official

- Machines should be emptied separately, and records kept of the cash from every machine. Wherever possible, the two officials who are responsible for this procedure should involve any club member and the count should never be done behind closed doors.

- For all emptying, a duplicate cash book should be used, and the date and the amount recorded with all members concerned signing that the figures are correct. If the cash is then handed to the steward for safe keeping or change then a receipt should be obtained.

- A separate book should be kept where the amounts taken are recorded together with the total at the end of the week. This book should also contain the meter readings of each machine. The meter readings should be calculated by the procedure shown below.

- Most modern machines have a 'coin in' meter and a 'coin out' meter and the digits are normally units of 10p or £1. In both cases the meter reading for the previous week is subtracted from the reading for this week. The balance for the 'coin out' meter is then deducted from the balance of the 'coin in' meter. Some gaming machines have £1 'coin in' and 10p 'coin out' meters so care should be taken to establish what the nominal profit is each week.

- It is very important that all the tubes or hoppers of the machine are filled to the same level each week from the cash boxes before the final count takes place. Unless this is done it will be impossible to reconcile the nominal profit with the actual takings.

By following this procedure, it is possible to spot any problems that may arise with any machine and its takings. The committee is also able to see which machine is performing best and whether any machine needs to be changed.

## Steward's Accommodation and Taxable Benefits

A large proportion of our clubs employ stewards who occupy residential accommodation, which is provided as part of the employment package. Over the years it has been made clear that it is essential, when dealing with employees who benefit from free accommodation, that any form of tenancy is avoided. Consequently, no money should be either received or deducted from such employees that could, in any view, be regarded as rent.

Club committees must, therefore, ensure that all employees who benefit from living accommodation do so as 'service occupiers.' An employee who occupies the club's property for the better performance of their duties – who is contractually required to do so and pays no rent–is a 'service occupier' and has no security of tenure. Such occupation ceases on termination of employment even if the termination is subsequently deemed to be unfair.

Steward occupation of club property is not a tenancy under the Landlord and Tenant Act and the terms of this Act do not apply to monies which are either deducted or charged in respect of the provision of heat and light. Some clubs and stewards have been shocked to discover that the supply of free heating and lighting provided by the club is regarded by HMRC as a taxable benefit. The fact is that this has always been accepted practice but in recent years the authorities have pursued such matters more rigorously.

The correct position is this: the club should include in its annual return to HMRC a declaration that it supplies free heat and light to the steward. The steward should include the information in their own annual income tax return. The declaration for payment for water is a "grey area." Some tax offices include this as a taxable benefit while others view the provision of water as part of providing the accommodation which is not taxable.

## Council Tax

At one time, tax inspectors advised clubs that when Council Tax was paid on a residential steward's accommodation by the club, this payment must be considered as a taxable benefit and should be declared on the steward's tax form P11D. In fact, the payment of Council Tax is NOT a taxable benefit.

Some clubs had to make backdated payments of tax on behalf of stewards when payment of Council Tax had not been declared while, in many cases, club stewards themselves had been paying tax on the benefit of having the Council Tax on their accommodation paid by the club.

In the event of being challenged in respect of Council Tax payments, clubs should quote Expenses and Benefits Tax Guide, 21.4, Section 145(4). The relevant section of the Guide reads–

> *'...no tax charges in respect of the provision of living accommodation will arise where–*
>
> - *it is necessary for the proper performance of the employee's duties that he, or she, should reside in the accommodation, or*
>
> - *the accommodation is provided for the better performance of the employee's duties and the employment is one of the kinds for which it is customary for employers to provide accommodation for the employee, or*
>
> - *there is a special threat to the employee's security, special security arrangements*

*are in force and the employee resides in the accommodation as part of those arrangements.'*

*'Where exemption is due in any of the above circumstances it also extends to any tax charge that might arise in respect of council tax reimbursed to, or paid on behalf of, the employee concerned.'*

## National Insurance

Clubs are reminded to ensure that National Insurance contributions are adjusted to consider increased payments of income tax due to taxable benefits. This will affect the employee's and the employer's contributions. In the past, National Insurance inspectors have not always been active in this particular area, but many clubs have been asked to complete and return information on the taxable benefits and if National Insurance contributions have not been adjusted to meet these increased payments, then backdated payments will be applied. National Insurance contributions are calculated on gross pay. Therefore, benefits which are not taxable, such as the provision of accommodation and the payment of council tax, will not be included within the calculation.

## Budgeting

Like any business, clubs must budget to ensure that finances are managed efficiently. Clubs are viewed as 'non-profit' making organisations. However, if a club does not set out to maximise the surplus on its activities, then it will never be able to develop and grow and may even have difficulty in meeting its regular maintenance costs. When budgeting, a club must set certain targets and the key to setting targets lies in the previous year's records and balance sheet.

In a small club, outgoings are made up mostly of the wages of the steward and any other staff, and of rent, rates, loan interest, insurance, heating, lighting, cleaning, bought-in supplies (drink, food, etc) and VAT. Total expenditure must be covered by total income, but a club needs to keep a check on its progress more regularly than once a year.

Some large organisations compare their income and expenditure weekly but for most clubs a monthly or quarterly check should be enough. Therefore, dividing annual expenditure by twelve or four will give the target figure which must be met from income every month or quarter. It is, of course, satisfying if income does cover outgoings at the end of a month, or quarter, but this is not the whole story.

Income will largely comprise subscriptions, bar sales, snooker room charges, gaming machine takings, lettings and other sales, and the income from these items will not be spread evenly over every month. Subscriptions tend to come in at one or two specific times during the year. Letting income is likely to be irregular and other items will vary between summer and winter. Similarly, some items of expenditure will also vary between one month and another.

For the sake of simplicity, let us suppose a club had a surplus last year of £5,000. The total expenditure was £100,000 and income was £105,000. The monthly target for this year is therefore £105,000 divided by twelve = £8,750. The accounts show that the net income proceeded along the lines set out in the following table–

|  | January-April | May | June | July | August | September |
|---|---|---|---|---|---|---|
| Income (£) | 36,600 | 8,900 | 8,550 | 6,200 | 4,900 | 6,900 |
| Target (£) | 35,000 | 8,750 | 8,750 | 8,750 | 8,750 | 8,750 |
| Period Deficit/ Surplus (£) | +1,600 | +250 | -200 | -2,550 | -3,850 | -1,850 |
| Cumulative Deficit/ Surplus (£) | +1,600 | +1,850 | +1,650 | -900 | -4,750 | -6,600 |

The figures indicate that the club's income has fallen during the summer months and that by September its deficit has become sufficiently significant to warrant attention. The committee must decide whether special action is required and what the action might be. One thing to note is that, while the deterioration began in June, the big drop in income took place in August. This might be expected when club activities and bar takings are likely to be below average. September showed a further deterioration, but at a much lower rate. Income will probably pick up in the last three months of the year.

The committee will be able to gain an idea of the possible trend for these months by looking at the same months in last year's accounts. If a surplus were recorded from October to December in that year, which would be enough to wipe out the accumulated deficit, no action may be needed. If the situation is unlikely to be resolved in that time, the committee will have to consider what must be done to correct the financial position. The importance of the target figure is that a warning has been given. The committee has not stumbled on in ignorance until an irresolvable situation has been reached, when the club might have to reduce the services it provides for members, or even to close.

Before deciding how to tackle a deteriorating position, the committee will have to take a closer look at some more detailed figures. Let us suppose that net figures for the months in question break down as shown in the following table–

| | January-April | May | June | July | August | September |
|---|---|---|---|---|---|---|
| Bar Takings (£) | 25,400 | 7,100 | 6,700 | 5,900 | 4,390 | 6,100 |
| Subscriptions (£) | 4,500 | 450 | – | 50 | – | – |
| Entertainments (£) | 4,800 | 800 | 700 | – | 310 | 300 |
| Lettings (£) | 1,100 | 470 | 900 | 200 | 50 | 300 |
| Other Sales (£) | 800 | 80 | 250 | 50 | 150 | 200 |

These figures need to be compared with the total and monthly figures for the previous year and the current monthly target. They indicate that bar income is well up to target and could exceed the previous year's total. Subscriptions have all been collect by July but income from the other three items is all lagging behind target, particularly lettings.

If the Committee now looks at the income under all headings for the preceding October to December, it will be able to see whether any recovery can be expected by the end of the year and if so, how great. If it does not expect to halt the decline in the club's finances, what should it do?

It can look at expenditure to see whether some economies are possible. Expenditure should be allocated under the same headings. Direct supplies have already been deducted from the calculations. Other costs will be on salaries, rent and rates, heating, lighting, cleaning, insurance, and bank interest, if any. Not all of these will be easily allocated to a heading.

The committee would be wise to give careful thought to the allocations. It is not good business to reduce the allocations to areas where income has been falling just to make the operations look better. The committee will have to choose how much of each cost is allocated to each income heading. While rent, rates and cleaning may be allocated according to the area of the club taken up by each income activity, staff and other costs will be allocated in different proportions.

In the example given, the expenditure allocations are likely to confirm the loss-making items. The committee now must choose what action is demanded to adjust the club's financial position. By producing a budget along these lines, the committee should be able to make its choices, and to make them in good time.

If there is no reason to anticipate a recovery in the remaining months of the year, there are several possibilities. The figures themselves will not give a definitive answer. The committee may consider that the running of dances or entertainment should be reduced, or charges increased. Another possibility is that subscriptions could be raised.

Yet again, the bar takings appear to be on course for a larger contribution to income than in the previous year, thereby creating an opportunity to allow bar income to subsidise the loss-making services for a time. This enables postponing any decision to raise charges or reduce entertainments. Eventually though, the necessity to put those other activities on a sound footing should be taken.

The above comments deal only with budgeting of the simplest kind. The club's accountant, financial adviser, or bank manager should be consulted on any matter concerning the club's finances on which the committee is uncertain.

## 7.0 EMPLOYMENT

### Introduction

Employment law is an area of law which is in an almost constant state of change and amendment and one which could easily take up an entire book, if not several volumes, on its own. In this chapter, I have addressed various matters relating to the basic principles of employment and provided some, hopefully useful, hints and tips to club committees. Often committee members find themselves, for the first time, in a position of management in respect of employees. The process of employing, managing, disciplining, and sometimes dismissing staff can be daunting.

The subject of employment has become a significant industry, created largely because of a decade of unprecedented new regulations. Whilst some of these new regulations may have been welcomed by businesses and unions, the fact is the cost to employers fighting employment tribunal claims is substantial. Around 30,000 legal actions – most claiming unfair dismissal, unequal pay, or sex discrimination – are filed with the employment tribunal service each year. Many of these claims are settled out of court but they still cost employers £7,000 on average, mainly in lawyers' fees.

It is essential for proper contracts, agreements, or terms and conditions of employment to be offered following the start of employment. The terms of employment need to be clearly set out and agreed between each party. Do not attempt to draft such documents yourself and do not use an old contract and attempt to amend it. A written statement of employment particulars is required by law as a minimum and must be given no later than two months after employment begins.

In case of doubt, or if there is any issue which arises that the committee is unsure of, seek advice. Most insurance policies now contain legal helplines as part of the normal cover and the insurance has been paid for, so use it! If advice is sought at the start of a dispute grievance with an employee and the advice from an insurance company is followed, then the policy will often underwrite the club against costs and damages if a claim of wrongful or unfair dismissal is successful. Bear in mind that employers should be reasonable and consistent when dealing with all employment issues.

## Working Time Regulations

The Working Time Regulations came into force in October 1998 and the basic rights and protections that the Regulations provide are–

- A limit of an average of forty-eight hours a week, which a worker can be required to work (though workers can choose to work more if they want to)

- A limit of an average of eight hours work in twenty-four, which night workers can be required to work

- A right for night workers to receive free health assessments

- A right to eleven hours rest a day (special conditions apply to employees who work split shifts)

- A right to one day off each week

- A right to an in-work rest break if the working day is longer than six hours

- A right to 4.8 weeks paid leave per year

## Holiday Pay

Employees, whether full-time or part-time, are legally entitled to 5.6 weeks paid annual leave. Additional annual leave may be agreed as part of a contract. A week's leave should allow employees to be away from work for a week i.e. it should be the same amount of time as the working week. If an employee works a five-day week, they are entitled to twenty-four days leave per annum. If an employee works a three-day week, the entitlement is 14.4 days leave per annum.

Employers can set the times that employees take their leave, for example for a Christmas shutdown. If an employment ends, the employee has a right to be paid for the leave time due and not taken. The Government increased the annual leave entitlement from 4.8 weeks to 5.6 weeks from 1 April 2009.

There is no statutory entitlement to paid leave for public holidays. Any right to paid time off for such holidays depends on the terms of the contract. If the contract does not specify this, the right to paid leave may have built up through custom and practice. Paid public holidays can be counted as part of the statutory 4.8 weeks' holiday entitlement under the Working Time Regulations 1998.

## National Minimum Wage

National Minimum Wage (NMW) applies to nearly all employees and sets hourly rates. The employer must maintain records of hours worked and payments made. The employee may request inspection of these records and ask for a copy of them. The rates set are based on the recommendations of the independent Low Pay Commission and they change on 1 October each year.

## Statutory Sick Pay

Employees who have been absent from work for at least four consecutive days are entitled to receive Statutory Sick Pay (SSP). This is known as the Period of Incapacity for Work (PIW). The four consecutive days can include days on which an employee is not required to work. Other qualifications are that the employee between the ages of sixteen and sixty-five and that the employee's average weekly earnings are above the Lower Earnings Limit. Many employees will have contracts providing payment whilst absent from work due to sickness, but if there are no provisions within the contract concerning additional Sick Pay then SSP only applies if the above qualifications are met.

Payments of SSP may be reclaimed by the employer via the employer's National Insurance Contributions (NICs). This scheme provides for full reimbursement of an employer's costs paid in any month where they exceed 13% of the employer's gross NICs for that month. SSP that is paid above the percentage threshold is recoverable in full. Employers will have to make a monthly calculation to see if they are eligible for a reclaim for that month. To work out whether any SSP is reclaimable an employer must:

- Calculate the gross NICs for the tax month, employees' primary and employer's secondary contributions (excluding any Class 1A liability)

- Multiply the figure of gross NICs by 13%
- Calculate the total SSP paid in the tax month

If the total SSP paid is greater than 13% of gross NICs, the employer can recover the difference.

## Notice Periods

A minimum period of notice is required to terminate the employment of an employee who has been employed for a qualifying period i.e. four weeks. The principal provisions are as follows–

To give rights to minimum periods of notice for termination of employment an employer is required to give an employee–

- At least one week's notice if the employee has been with him continuously for four weeks or more, but not exceeding two years

- At least one week's notice for each year of continuous employment if his period of continuous employment is two years or more, but less than twelve years

- At least twelve weeks' notice if his period of continuous employment is twelve years or more

## Redundancy

Employees are entitled to redundancy payments if they are dismissed due to one of the following–

- The employer has ceased, or intends to cease, to carry on the business for the purposes of which the employee was so employed

- The employer has ceased, or intends to cease, to carry on the business in the place where the employee was so employed

- The requirements of the business for employees to carry out work of a particular kind has ceased or diminished or are expected to cease or diminish

- The requirements of the business for the employees to carry out work of a particular kind, in the place where they were so employed, has ceased, or diminished or are expected to cease or diminish

Employees have the right to a lump sum payment if dismissed because of redundancy. The amount is related to age, length of continuous service and weekly pay up to a maximum. The employer must also provide a written statement showing how the payment has been calculated at or before the time it is paid. Any dispute about whether a redundancy payment is due, or about its size, can be determined by an employment tribunal.

Employers should use objective criteria, wherever possible, that is precisely defined and capable of being applied in an independent way when selecting employees for redundancy. This is to ensure that employees are not selected unfairly. The chosen criteria should be consistently applied by all employers, irrespective of size. There should also be an appeals procedure. Examples of such criteria are–

- Attendance record (if this is fully accurate and reasons for and extent of absence are known)
- Disciplinary record (if this is fully accurate)
- Skills or experience
- Standard of work performance
- Aptitude for work

Formal qualifications and advanced skills should be considered, but not in isolation.

Clubs must take care, in all cases of redundancy, not to create a situation where unfair dismissal can be claimed.

## Maternity Leave

Pregnant women have statutory maternity rights and employees should be made aware of what those rights are. Employees must inform the club of any pregnancy as soon as possible.

## Standard Maternity Rights

Employees with less than twenty-six weeks' service at the end of the fifteenth week before the Expected Week of Childbirth (EWC) will be entitled to the following benefits–

## Time off for Ante-Natal Care

All employees, regardless of length of service, have the right to reasonable time off for ante-natal care. An employee will be entitled to be paid for her periods of absence at her appropriate hourly rate.

To qualify for paid leave to attend the first ante-natal appointment, an employee must be pregnant and have made an appointment to receive ante-natal care on the advice of a registered medical practitioner, registered midwife, or registered health visitor. To obtain paid time off work to attend subsequent ante-natal appointments, the employee must provide their manager with the following in advance of any appointments–

- A certificate of pregnancy from a registered medical practitioner, registered midwife, or registered health visitor, and

- An appointment card or some other document(s) showing that the appointment has been made

## Length of Maternity Leave

Employees are entitled to twenty-six weeks' maternity leave, called Ordinary Maternity Leave (OML). OML can begin at any time after the beginning of the eleventh week before the EWC. During OML, the employee will, except for remuneration, be entitled to the benefit of the terms and conditions of employment that would have been applicable to her had she not been on maternity leave.

The employee must notify the club of an intention to take OML before the fifteenth week as above before the EWC. The club is required to respond within twenty-eight days giving the date when the employee is expected to return to work after taking their full maternity leave entitlement. Employees will be able to change their mind about the date on which they want their leave to start providing they notify the club; such notification being received by the club at least twenty-eight days in advance (unless this is not reasonably practicable).

## Maternity Allowance (MA)

Employees with less than twenty-six weeks' service are not entitled to Statutory Maternity pay but may qualify for a Maternity Allowance (MA), payable by the Benefits Agency for a maximum period of absence of twenty-six weeks. Information on the details of eligibility for MA and the amounts payable should be sought from the Benefits Agency.

## Right to Return

Subject to statutory provision, the employee has the right to return to work at the end of the OML period. If the employee wishes to return to work before the end of her OML period, she must give her manager at least twenty-eight days' notice in writing of the date on which she intends to return. The employee will not be allowed to return to work within two weeks after the date of birth.

## Additional Maternity Rights

Employees who have completed at least twenty-six weeks' continuous employment by the fifteenth week before the EWC will, in addition to Standard Maternity Rights, be entitled to the following benefits–

## Statutory Maternity Pay (SMP)

Statutory Maternity Pay (SMP) is payable for a maximum period of twenty-six weeks beginning at any time from the eleventh week before the EWC. SMP is payable at a higher rate for the first six weeks of absence with the rate being 90% of the employee's normal weekly pay. Normal weekly pay means average basic pay over the eight weeks up to the fifteenth week before the EWC. For any further weeks of absence up to the maximum SMP period, the employee is paid at the rate fixed by the Government.

The right to SMP is conditional upon the employee–

- Producing Form MAT1B indicating the expected date of her confinement signed by a registered midwife or medical doctor to her group head/manager, and

- Giving at least twenty-eight days' notice in writing of her intended absence due to pregnancy unless it is not reasonably practicable for her to do so

## Additional Maternity Leave (AML)

AML starts immediately after the OML period, continues for a further twenty-six weeks and is unpaid. AML can be extended for a further four weeks in special circumstances, such as a pregnancy related illness, or by taking parental leave. If the employee does not intend to take AML or wishes to return to work before the end of her AML, she must give twenty-eight days' notice to the club of her intended date of return.

## Right to return to work after AML

Subject to statutory provision, the employee has the right to return to work at the end of the AML period. During AML, the employee will, except for remuneration, be entitled to the benefits of the terms and conditions of employment that would have been applicable had she not been on leave. If the employee does not intend to return to work at the end of her maternity leave, she must give the club proper notice, as provided in her contract of employment.

## Paternity Leave

### Standard Paternity Rights

Employees who become fathers are entitled to take paternity leave. To qualify, an employee must–

- Have or expect to have responsibility for the child's upbringing
- Be the biological father of the child or the mother's husband or partner
- Have worked continuously for their employer for twenty-six weeks by the fifteenth week before the baby is due

The employee must confirm that he meets these eligibility conditions in writing.

### Length of Paternity Leave

Eligible employees will be entitled to take two consecutive weeks' paternity leave. They can choose to start their leave–

- From the date of the child's birth (whether this is earlier or later than expected), or
- From a chosen number of days or weeks after the date of the child's birth (whether this is earlier or later than expected), or
- From a chosen date

Leave can start on any day of the week on or following the child's birth but must be completed–

- Within fifty-six days of the actual date of birth of the child, or
- If the child is born early, within the period from the actual date of birth up to fifty-six days after the EWC

Only one period of leave will be available to employees irrespective of whether more than one child is born as the result of the same pregnancy.

### Statutory Paternity Pay (SPP)

During their paternity leave, most employees will be entitled to Statutory Paternity Pay (SPP). SPP will be paid by employers for either one or two consecutive weeks as the employee has chosen. The rate of SPP will be the same as the standard rate of SMP (see above).

**Parental Leave**

Employees are entitled by law to unpaid leave to look after young children or newly adopted children. An employee will qualify for this right if they have been continuously employed for one year or more and–

- Is the parent (named on the birth certificate) of a child who is under five years old, or

- Has adopted a child under the age of eighteen (the right lasts for five years from the date on which the child is placed for adoption or until the child's eighteenth birthday, whichever is the sooner), or

- Has taken on formal parental responsibility for a child who is under five years old, (a stepparent will have to apply to court to acquire formal parental responsibility if they wish to take parental leave in respect of their spouse's children)

Parental leave is available to both parents and is unpaid.

**Length of Parental Leave**

An employee is entitled to thirteen weeks' unpaid leave in respect of each child and twenty-one days' notice of taking leave must be given. Employees may take leave in blocks of no less than one week (this minimum period does not apply in relation to a child with a disability) and may not take more than four weeks' leave in respect of any individual child during a particular year. The club can postpone leave for up to six months for business reasons.

**Disciplinary and Grievance Procedures**

Disciplinary action and handling grievances are the two main areas where employers make mistakes. The reason for this is often due to committees dealing with employees inconsistently. The management of staff sometimes requires employees having to be told that their work, conduct, or timekeeping is unsatisfactory. The danger of these matters being dealt with by committee is that no single person wishes to confront staff and consequently problems are left unmanaged to the point when committees overreact and rush into warnings or dismissals. Equally, club employees find that, without a proper system of management in place, any grievances which they may have are not dealt with and this can often be a cause of dissatisfaction.

Employees are more likely to accept workplace rules if it is explained why such rules are necessary. Matters such as conduct, timekeeping, absence, health and safety, performance and behaviour should be clearly set out and agreed. Employment terms should also specify offences which would be regarded as gross misconduct, such as theft, fraud or violence that would result in dismissal without notice.

Proper disciplinary and grievance procedures, which are clearly set out within contracts, agreements and terms and conditions of employment, help employees achieve and maintain acceptable standards of work and help to avoid confrontation between the committee and club employees.

Formal disciplinary procedures are normally implemented in the following stages–

- First formal verbal warning for misconduct or unsatisfactory performance
- First formal written warning
- Second and final written warning
- Dismissal or other sanction

There must be a procedure in place which permits employees to appeal against any disciplinary action. Such appeals must be heard by persons who were not part of the original disciplinary procedure.

All employers are required to follow a minimum three stage statutory procedure for dealing with all employment issues including dismissal and handling grievances. The three steps are–

1. Inform the employer of the grievance in writing.
2. Meet to discuss the grievance and
3. Hold an appeal, if requested.

Employment tribunals are entitled to adjust any award of compensation by between ten and fifty percent for failure to implement the above procedure.

Grievance procedures should be adopted to achieve a settlement on any disputes as quickly, fairly, and efficiently as possible; they should be included in all contracts, agreements and terms and conditions of employment.

Unfair dismissal claims may only be made if an employee has been continuously employed for at least one year at the time of dismissal. Employees with less than one year's service, who are dismissed on the grounds of sex, race, religion or belief, sexual orientation, age, or disability, may bring claims for discriminatory dismissal under the relevant legislation irrespective of length of service.

## Stewards

As one of the main sources of revenue in a club is the bar, it is essential that it should be managed efficiently and run on strict business lines. A material factor in the bar's successful conduct lies in the appointment of the right person as steward.

The steward's duties should be clearly defined. The steward is responsible for the premises and before each session when the club is opened should make sure an inspection of all the rooms to ensure they are clean and tidy. The steward should supervise other employees who work behind the bar since the stock and takings are the steward's responsibility.

All employees, however, are under the full control of the committee and are bound to carry out the legal orders of that body. It is the committee who are ultimately responsible for club employees and have sole authority of appointment and dismissal. It must therefore be understood by the steward that, although other employees work under their supervision, they are employed by the committee on behalf of the club.

The principal duties of the steward are–

- To see that the club premises are opened and closed as provided for in the rules and that the registered hours for the supply of intoxicants are strictly observed

- To see that a record of all goods received is kept and entered in the 'Goods Received' book for checking with tradesmen's invoices

- To see that the exact amount of each day's takings is entered in the 'Steward's Daily Takings' book and the money banked (the Secretary, Treasurer and Finance Sub-Committee should check this book at least once a week)

- To liaise closely with the club's Secretary and to bring to the Secretary's attention any matter relating to the club's business or of any known beach of the club's rules

- To see that persons not entitled to be on the club's premises are asked to leave and that persons who are not entitled to be supplied with intoxicating liquor are not served

- To be present when the stock is arranged that the various articles may be easily recorded

It is incompatible with the membership of a club for an employee to be a member of the club they serve. There is a clear conflict of interests which is likely to lead to problems between management and staff. For example, if an employee is permitted either to become or remain a member of the club then such a person is also entitled to enjoy the rights of membership which, in such cases, include the right to vote at meetings and be nominated for office. If employees/members are elected to the committee then they are in the unacceptable position of being both their own employer at the same time as being the other members' employees. Even as members, such employees have voting and nomination rights and consequently can have influence in general meetings over management affairs.

Many stewards give the impression that they are the club's licensee. However, this is not the case. It is the club itself, as an organised group or body, to which the Club Premises Certificate (CPC) is granted. This confusion often arises when a steward has previously run a pub and inadvertently believes that the same principles apply.

Obviously, a steward who is a good 'mein host' is an asset to any club. Members like being welcomed to their club and new members and guests are often particularly encouraged to use the club more frequently if a friendly face is running the bar. However, experience has shown that this situation should not continue to the extent that in management terms 'the tail is wagging the dog.'

## Recruiting a Steward

Before you place an advertisement to recruit a new steward, you need to look at one or two issues about why you have a vacancy at all and why your last steward left. People sometimes leave their jobs for good reasons, but a little detective work might reveal that your conditions of employment do not encourage people to give you long-term commitment.

You might even find that the way you recruited last time fell short of the mark and you lost the last steward because they were the wrong choice in the first place. If this is the case, regard the current vacancy as a chance to get the recruitment procedure right.

Examine in detail exactly what the job of steward entails. This might be a good time to restructure the job if necessary. Write a list of all the duties required. They will fall quite naturally into four or five main areas such as customer service, cleaning and maintenance, stock control or staff management. Finer detail can then be recorded under these headings.

When you have completed this job description, you can write down what knowledge and skills are required for someone to do the job well. Examples of this might be knowledge of bar stock control procedures or the skill of handling customers or members. What you will be creating is a list of the abilities you should be looking for in the ideal candidate. You might also add to this list some of the other things that you should be looking for which are more specific, such as availability to work the hours required.

Devising a concise advertisement based on your specifications will make it clear what the job entails and can indicate the attributes which are considered essential for success in the post. Be careful not to fall foul of discrimination law. You cannot state that you do or do not want a particular sex or racial group for the job. Put a closing date on applications so that you can compare all your candidates and arrange to see the best ones.

Advertising by word of mouth and using personal recommendations can be very effective and it is certainly cheap. However, this approach does have its problems. It can be tempting to compromise for convenience sake when a reasonable candidate is introduced to you by a personal contact. It can also cause offence if you decide to reject someone recommended to you. Even worse, taking on someone's friend or relative, only to have to dismiss them later because they turned out to be unsuitable, can be damaging to staff or personal relationships.

When you have received application forms and CVs, compare what each of the candidates has to offer to the specification you had put together at the outset of this recruitment campaign. If you want customer relations skills, what evidence is there in the application of experience of this in previous employment? If you want a good organiser, where can evidence of this be seen in the type of work that the applicant has been doing?

Remember to look for obvious problems such as gaps in employment history or changes of job which seem hard to explain (for example, giving up a lucrative land lordship or club steward position somewhere else).

Never leave the interview itself just to one person from a club. Convene an interviewing panel from the committee. Alternatively, have one person interview the applicants and then pass them on to a second stage interviewer. Two opinions will help to obviate personal bias and maximise the possibility of an objective decision.

The application or CV can only provide prompts for in depth investigation; it cannot give you a comprehensive picture on its own. Do not miss the opportunity to find out about what the candidate is capable of by enquiring thoroughly about the way they are doing their present job or their experience in any other employment. Every interviewee should be asked to demonstrate that they have the skills and abilities that you require and question how their past experience relates to your specific requirements. How, for example, have they dealt with running a profitable bar, handling difficult staff issues, building relationships with customers or members, and dealing with contractors? You should be able to find out in the interview if the applicant matches your requirements.

Check the provenance of any referees you are given. Former employers are best, and you can check that they do in fact exist as bona fide sources of information. Personal referees have limited value as they would hardly have been offered if they were not expected to give glowing praise.

Ask the referee questions which help them tell you what you need to know about reliability, efficiency, customer relations and trustworthiness. Referees have a duty of care to give you truthful facts about your candidate. If they find it hard to give you constructive feedback, they might decline to write anything or keep to the barest of facts, such as dates of employment. Make sure you telephone all referees to validate their references. When you offer employment, remember to make it conditional on any checks you must make. You may need to make such a conditional offer to approach a current employer. Never approach referees without the candidate's express permission.

The process comes full circle at the decision stage. Compare what your most promising candidate has to offer against what you say that you require in your specification. If you do not find that person this time around, you would be better to start again rather than make an appointment that is only second best.

## General

## Accident to Paid Employees

The Common Law liability of employers for injuries to their employees is unlimited in amount. The grounds upon which an employee may make a claim are extensive. For example, an employer may be successfully proceeded against by an employee injured through the negligence of a fellow employee with a consequent award of damages. Each employer shall hold and display a certificate of insurance certifying that he is covered under the terms of the Employers Liability (Compulsory Insurance) Act 1969.

## 8.0 HEALTH & SAFETY
### What is Health and Safety at Work?

Occupational Health and Safety is about keeping people safe and healthy whilst at work. It is about ensuring that employers and employees know their responsibilities and play their part in ensuring that hazards and risks to health and safety at work are identified and either eliminated or reduced to an acceptable level.

*Section 2 of the Health and Safety at Work Act 1974 (HSWA)* requires all employers to put in place systems of work which ensure, so far as is reasonably practicable, that employees may work without risk to their safety.

*Section 3, paragraph 3 of The Management of Health and Safety at Work Regulations 1999* passed under HSWA impose an absolute obligation on employers to put in place suitable and sufficient risk assessments for the risks facing their employees. These assessments must be reviewed whenever there is a significant change in risk exposure.

### Legal requirements

In operating your club, you must comply with the Health and Safety at Work Act 1974.

The Health and Safety at Work Act 1974 (and associated Regulations) place legal duties on employers, employees, self-employed persons, and occupiers of buildings in which people who are not their own employees work.

The Regulations include:

*COSHH* – Control of Substances Hazardous to Health.

*RIDDOR* – Reporting of Injuries, Diseases and Dangerous Occurrences Regulations.

### Employers' responsibilities include:

• Safeguarding of health and safety of employees, non-employees, and visitors – anyone whose health and safety might be affected by the operation of the business

- Consulting with employees

- Providing personal protective equipment (PPE) where appropriate

- Provision of free training in health and safety for staff

- Appointing competent persons to take charge of health and safety, fire safety and first aid in the workplace

- First aid facilities

- Welfare facilities

- Health and safety policies where required

- The provision of safe systems of work, a safe environment, ensuring the safe handling, storage, and movement of loads, substances, and chemicals

- Carrying out risk assessments as appropriate

Health and Safety Policy – Every employer who employs five employees or more must have a written Health and Safety policy and must review and revise that policy on a regular basis.

The policy must contain three main parts:

1. A general statement of health and safety intentions – what the policy is intended to achieve.

2. Organisation and accountability – explaining how the provision of health and safety will be delivered and identifying who has responsibility for the various elements of health and safety policy, who they report to and who is accountable in the event of a failure of policy or practice.

3. Practical arrangement – information communicated to employees concerning the systems and procedures that ensure the safe conduct of working practices.

### Employees' responsibilities include:

- Taking reasonable care of themselves and others by ensuring their behaviour does not put themselves or others unnecessarily at risk

- Co-operating with their employer in implementing safe systems of work

- Not to misuse or act with reckless intent in respect of anything that is used to deliver a healthy and safe working environment

- Complying with the Health and Safety at Work Act, COSHH and RIDDOR

- Report any health and safety issues (such as faulty equipment, hazards, missing guards) accidents and near misses or ill-health
- To correctly use PPE and report any defective or missing PPE

**Self-employed persons responsibilities include:**

- Taking care of their own health and safety
- Taking care of the health and safety of other people who may be affected by their work tasks

In a social club self-employed people would include anyone to whom you have sub-contracted the provision of catering, or people engaged in providing entertainment in your club or providing maintenance services.

**Occupiers of buildings responsibilities include:**

- Responsibility to exercise a duty of care towards people working in buildings they control even if those persons are not their employees

In a club this might include renting part of the building as an office to another organisation.

**Enforcement**

Health and safety law is enforced either by:

- The Health and Safety Executive (HSE), or
- The local authority Environmental Health Officer (EHO)

*HSE* – inspectors responsible for factories, hospitals, and schools etc.

*EHO* – shops offices, social clubs, public houses, warehouses etc.

Inspectors have powers to gain access to workplaces at reasonable times; order that the scene of an accident remains intact for inspection purposes; collect evidence; can ask questions, give advice, and remove and test equipment.

Prosecutions for breaches of Health and Safety law only take place as a last resort. Usually Inspectors or EHOs will give written advice, or in more serious cases serve either:

- An Improvement Notice requiring corrective action by a given date, or
- A Prohibition Notice when there is a risk of serious injury and work or a particular work activity must cease immediately

Criminal prosecutions against an employer can follow serious health and safety law breaches or the failure to comply with an Improvement or Prohibition Notice. Penalties can range from a small fine to two years' imprisonment and/or an unlimited fine.

## The role and purpose of risk assessments

The purpose of a risk assessment is to identify hazards, assess the probability of harm arising out of the risks posed by nay hazards that are identified and to prescribe measures that can be taken either to eliminate a risk or reduce it to an acceptable level.

The overall purpose of risk assessments is simply to ensure that the working environment is as safe as it can possibly be. Risk assessment is at the heart of health and safety legislation and to the creation and maintenance of a safe working environment.

## When is risk assessment needed?

Employers must assess and manage health and safety risks, regardless of whether the employer is operating a large or a small business. Risk assessments are needed wherever processes of work are in operation that might pose hazards for employees or others who might reasonably be expected to be affected by the operation of the business.

In a social club you will operate a kitchen, a beer cellar and a bar. Members and guests have access to the premises for social purposes and contractors or delivery workers may need temporary access to your club. All these activities have the potential to create hazards and harms and need to be risk-assessed.

A risk assessment is an important tool in protecting workers and the club. It helps you focus on those risks that have the potential to cause harm. Most of these risks can be eliminated or reduced by straightforward control measures.

Once a risk assessment has been completed the results need to be put into practice. Improvements can be implemented by an action plan that gives priority to the elimination or reduction of the most significant risks.

Specific assessments are a legal requirement:

- If a woman informs her employer that she is pregnant
- When a person aged between 16 and 18 years is employed

The five stages to risk assessment

1. Identify the hazards
2. Identify who may be harmed

3. Evaluate the risks and consider whether existing precautions are sufficient

4. Record your findings

5. Review and revise as necessary

Step 1: identify the hazard – you need only consider those hazards that could reasonably be expected to result in a significant harm. For example:

- Slipping or tripping hazards
- Chemicals
- Fumes or dust
- Plant, machinery or moving vehicles
- High or low temperatures
- Manual handling operations
- Noise
- Repetitive processes, particularly those that control the pace of work
- Work-related stress

Step 2: identify who may be harmed – consider who is likely to be affected by the operation of your club, or of the particular process that you are assessing. This will include:

- Employees
- Outside contractors
- Visitors or members of the public, including members or guests who might be affected by the operation of the club
- People who might be particularly vulnerable – pregnant women, disabled persons, inexperienced or young workers

Step 3: Evaluate the risks and consider whether existing precautions are sufficient – consider whether the risks are already adequately controlled. If they are not, then you must consider the likelihood of these risks leading to significant harm and introduce adequate control measures to eliminate or reduce the risk to an acceptable level. Consider the following:

- Can the hazard be eliminated, or its cause mitigated by a change of process that reduces risk, such as limiting the time-exposure of workers to the hazard?

- Can the hazard be isolated or enclosed in such a way as to limit the exposure of persons to it?
- Would appropriate training reduce the risks?
- Would the provision of PPE reduce the risk?
- Could the likelihood of serious harm be mitigated by the provision of first aid facilities?

Step 4: Record the findings – best practice is always to document a risk assessment; this ensures that you can demonstrate due diligence and legal compliance in the event of an accident and subsequent investigation. If a club has five or more employees, recording all risk assessments is a legal requirement.

Step 5: review and revise as necessary – risk assessments should be reviewed periodically and in particular if there has been an accident or near miss or changes have occurred in the workplace.

### Employees and risk assessments

It is advisable to consult employees most likely to be affected when conducting a risk assessment. Once completed, employees have a responsibility to follow the recommendations of the risk assessment concerned.

### Fire safety

Every business must appoint a Fire Marshal to take charge of fire safety arrangements in the workplace. The Fire Marshal can also carry out a fire risk assessment, using the 'five steps to risk assessment' model.

### Common causes of fire include:

- Accumulation of combustibles (bags of rubbish etc)
- Faulty electrical equipment
- Arson (fires started as a deliberate criminal act)
- Flammable products used in the company's processes
- Cooking (e.g., deep fat fryers)
- Hot liquids
- Naked flames

For a fire to start there must be a process of combustion that involves three elements:

1.  Oxygen – mostly this is provided from the air, although it may on occasion come from another sources, e.g., a tank of oxygen.
2.  Heat – is what sparks ignition, e.g., a discarded cigarette, a faulty plug.
3.  Fuel – anything that burns, e.g., paper, wood, hot fat.

Reducing risks – measures that reduce the risk of fires starting, or of causing injury and death if they do start include:

*   Good housekeeping to control the three elements of fire
*   Systems for detecting and warning of fire, including smoke detectors and fire alarm points
*   Safe means of escape with correct green signage for fire evacuations to take place. There should always be alternative evacuation routes
*   Fire doors to limit the spread of fire
*   Fire exit doors that can be easily opened from the inside and which open outwards
*   Fire escapes from upper floors

Fire-fighting equipment – includes:

*   Sprinkler systems
*   Fire extinguishers

Employees should be trained in the proper use of fire extinguishers.

Fire safety procedures – all employees and occupants of a building must have received adequate instruction about what to do in the event of a fire emergency. A Fire Emergency Evacuation Plan must be provided by the employer and this should be rehearsed regularly in a Fire Practice.

## What is COSHH?

COSHH is an acronym that stands for 'Control of Substances Hazardous to Health'. It is the law that requires employers to control substances that are hazardous to health. You can prevent or reduce workers' exposure to hazardous substances by:

*   Finding out what the health hazards are
*   Deciding how to prevent harm to health

- Providing control measures to reduce harm to health
- Making sure they are used
- Keeping all control measures in good working order
- Providing information, instruction and training for employees and others
- Providing monitoring and health surveillance in appropriate cases
- Planning for emergencies

Most clubs use substances, or products that are mixtures of substances. Some of these could cause harm to employees, contractors, and other people.

Sometimes substances are easily recognised as harmful. Common substances such as paint, bleach, drain unblocking products, beer line cleaner and carbon dioxide used in the beer cellar, or dust from natural materials may also be harmful.

COSHH also covers **asphyxiating gases.**

COSHH covers germs that cause diseases such as leptospirosis and legionnaires disease arising out of air conditioning systems/

COSHH **does not cover** lead, asbestos or radioactive substances because these have their own specific regulations.

**RIDDOR reporting requirements**

You are required to report certain matters to the HSE. The regulations under which accidents and dangerous occurrences must be reported are known as 'RIDDOR': Reporting of Incidents, Diseases or Dangerous Occurrences Regulations 1995. Under these Regulations there is a legal duty placed on employers, self-employed people and people in control of premises to report work-related fatalities, major injuries or injuries that result in over-three-days off work, work related diseases and dangerous occurrences.

The responsible person must make an online report to the Incident Contact Centre at the HSE where you can access a suite of seven forms available on HSE's website: **www.hse.gov.uk**

Failure to report these incidents is a criminal offence and your enforcing authority could prosecute offenders which may result in fines of up to £5,000 in the Magistrates' court. Conviction in the Crown Court carries an unlimited fine. Incidents and dangerous occurrences that should be reported include:

- Work-related deaths (immediately)

- Major injuries, such as broken limbs (immediately)
- Over-three-day-injuries where the worker is away from work or unable to perform their duties for more than three consecutive days
- Injuries to members of the public or people not at work who are taken from the scene to hospital
- Work-related diseases, and
- Dangerous occurrences (near misses)

Time scales for reporting these occurrences vary, but 'best practice' is to report any of the above immediately.

## COVID-19

In 2020 we saw the advent of a viral pandemic that involved a novel corona virus - 'COVID-19'. This is a respiratory illness that is spread by infected droplets. There are two main ways in which it spreads:

- Where droplets are left on surfaces such as tables or door handles and another person touches these surfaces and transfers the virus by their hands touching their mouth or eyes
- Aerosol transmission – whereby sneezing, coughing or even singing or loud talking can send droplets through the air which are then breathed in by other people.

Frequent and thorough hand washing lasting for at least 20 seconds is an important protection against transmission of the virus.

To reduce the speed of transmission and the incidence of COVID-19 in the population the UK government at Westminster and the devolved administrations in Scotland, Wales and Northern Ireland instigated a variety of control measures, which included the requirement for many businesses to cease operating and shut down. This included the social club sector and other sectors that sold food and drink for consumption on the premises, such as pubs, bars, restaurants, and nightclubs. From 4 July 2020 social clubs, pubs, bars, and restaurants, were allowed to reopen provided they were able to do so in a COVID-19 secure manner.

The starting point for social clubs re-opening safely is the Department for Business, Enterprise, and Industrial Strategy (BEIS) "5 steps to working safely" guidance.

The preamble to the BEIS Working Safely Guidance requires consideration of all the guides relevant to the workplace in question. The 5 steps are:

1. Carry out a COVID-19 risk assessment.

2. Develop cleaning, handwashing, and hygiene procedures.

3. Help people work from home.

4. Maintain 2m social distancing, where possible.

5. Where people cannot be 2m apart, manage risk

The COVID-19 risk assessment guidance can be found on the HSE website and includes specific guidance on "Working safely during the coronavirus (COVID19) outbreak" including the undertaking of risk assessments. It follows, therefore, that risk assessment should be undertaken in line with HSE and the Working Safely Guidance.

**Steps that will usually be needed**

• Calculating the maximum number of customers that can reasonably follow social distancing guidelines (2m, or 1m with risk mitigation where 2m is not viable, is acceptable) at the club.

• Taking into account total indoor and outdoor space, specific club characteristics such as furniture as well as likely pinch points and busy areas.

• Reconfiguring indoor and outdoor seating and tables to maintain social distancing guidelines (2m, or 1m with risk mitigation where 2m is not viable, is acceptable) between members/guests of different households or support bubbles. For example, increasing the distance between tables.

- Working with your local authority or landlord to take into account the impact of your processes, including queues, on public spaces such as high streets and public car parks.

- Working with neighbouring businesses and local authorities to provide additional parking or facilities such as bike-racks, where possible, to help members and guests avoid using public transport.

- Reducing the need for members and guests to queue, but where this is unavoidable, discouraging them from queueing indoors and using outside spaces for queueing where available and safe. For example, using some car parks and existing outdoor services areas.

- Providing clear guidance on social distancing and hygiene to people on arrival, for example, signage, visual aids and before arrival, such as by phone, on the website or by email.

- Managing the entry of members and guests, and their number at the club, so that all indoor members and guests are seated with appropriate distancing, and those outdoors have appropriately spaced seating or standing room. This is to ensure that the club, including areas of congestion does not become overcrowded. Managing entry numbers can be done, for example, through reservation systems, social distancing markings, having people queue at a safe distance for toilets or bringing payment machines to people, where possible.

- Managing outside queues to ensure they do not cause a risk to individuals, other businesses or additional security risks, for example by introducing queuing systems, having staff direct members and guests and protecting queues from traffic by routing them behind permanent physical structures such as street furniture, bike racks, bollards or putting up barriers.

- Making members and guests aware of, and encouraging compliance with, limits on gatherings. For example, on arrival or at booking. Indoor gatherings are limited to members of any two households (or support bubbles), while outdoor gatherings are limited to members of any two households (or support bubbles), or a group of at most six people from any number of households.

**Note:** Members and guests seated inside a club's premises are not regarded as a 'gathering', but as a collection of gatherings, so there is no limit on the total number of people allowed inside the premises except as indicated by your own risk assessment designed to create a COVID-19 secure operation.

It is likely that precautions to limit the risk of transmitting COVID-19 may have to be in place for some time. It is important that social clubs create an environment in which members and guests feel safe if clubs are to continue to operate successfully in the future. Member clubs can access a digital risk assessment tool via the ACC website to assist them in deciding what measures they need to take in their premises to make them COVID-19 secure.

## 9.0 RULES AND REGULATIONS

### Rules and Byelaws

The rules of any club represent a contract between the members with each other, and in the case of an incorporated club between the members and the club.

On election to membership, a person is legally held to agree with the rules and regulations in force and is presumed to have full knowledge of them. Ignorance thereafter is no defence.

The rules set out the conduct expected of the committee and the members and the committee's authority is determined by the rules. These powers are binding and should be clearly set out. Decisions made by the committee, in accordance with the club's rules, cannot be over-ridden by a General Meeting of members.

The committee's powers are generally wide. They encompass administrative functions, such as ordering supplies, deciding on new buildings, or dealing with alterations to the premises. Committees may also have quasi-judicial functions. These include how to discipline a member who has broken a club rule or been guilty of criminal offences outside the club. In reaching their decisions, the committee must act judicially: they must act in good faith, following the rules of natural justice and the club rules when determining disputes.

Committees may also have the power to make byelaws or regulations affecting the club. Again, they cannot act outside the rules, or in a manner inconsistent with them. It must also be stressed that Private Members' Clubs are not immune from the law and public policy, either as expressed in the rules and regulations or in statute law.

Any person elected to a club committee should therefore apply themselves to study the rules of the club and the rules of procedure. This will enable them to meet the needs of the club, and to use their voice and vote for the good of their fellow members.

Satisfactory rules are the road to an efficient club. They should plainly provide for the committee to be elected by the club membership and for the committee to serve at the pleasure of the members. They should also provide for members to be able to alter them.

Subscriptions should be provided for by stating that they may be fixed at an amount to be determined by the membership in General Meeting or that the committee may determine the actual sum from time to time.

A further issue to be settled in the rules is the manner of any appeal against a decision of the committee on disciplinary matters. This may be by arbitration or by any members selected by the committee to decide such appeals. There should, however, be no appeal from decisions taken by the committees in day-to-day management matters, such as the employment or dismissal of staff, or the use of funds as permitted by the rules.

If members do not care for the way their club is managed, then the remedy is for them to ensure that the rules contain a proper procedure for the removal of the offending officers and/or committee members, either individually or collectively.

The rules also provide protection against dictatorship. It appears that, at times, some officers or committees do believe that they are unchallengeable, but this is not so. As already stated, they must not act ultra vires (outside the rules), and those same rules should contain all that is necessary for the membership to be able to remove offending officials. It is to be hoped that such a step will never be taken lightly. The greatest safeguard against such an eventuality is to take the utmost care in choosing those who will serve on the committee. But no choice can be guaranteed to be infallible.

Mistakes do occur, and the time may arise when a committee is hopelessly at odds with the feelings of the body of the membership, or the behaviour of one committee member attracts continued criticism. There is always the possibility that a committee will fail to deal correctly with matters of discipline and the member concerned may consider he has been treated unfairly.

A committee may not act contrary to the law or the rules of natural justice. 'Natural justice' may reasonably be summarised as the rules and procedures to be followed by any person or body charged with the duty of adjudicating upon disputes between the rights of others.

A committee must act in good faith and without bias, giving each party an adequate opportunity to state their case and to hear the arguments of the other party. An aggrieved member should be able to find their remedy within club rules since most provide for arbitration in the event of a dispute. If these do not exist, they have the right to take their case to the courts.

Where a committee is required to hear a complaint against one of their own members, that member should immediately withdraw from any deliberations of the committee. It is a simple tenet of natural justice that no one should sit as judge and jury in his or her own case. The same consideration applies where a committee member is directly involved in a complaint against some other club member. As an interested party in the outcome of the hearing, the committee member should take no part in the discussions of the complaint.

The committee must be given enough powers by or under the rules, and in enough detail for it to be able to manage the club effectively. Ambiguity or deficiencies in the rules can only lead to muddled administration and possible disputes.

## Alteration of Rules

The rules of a club can only be amended in accordance with the provisions of its rule or rules governing such matters. Where any alteration is made in the rules of a club, the Secretary must give written notice of the alteration to the Licensing Authority. The Secretary is liable to a fine if the notice required is not given within twenty-eight days of the alteration. In the case of clubs registered under the Industrial and Provident Societies Acts and the Friendly Societies Acts, no amendment of rules is valid until registered by the Financial Services Authority. The twenty-eight days' notice, therefore, operates from the date of registration of the amendment.

## Inter-Affiliation Ticket Scheme

Almost all club organisations and associations operate reciprocal arrangement schemes whereby members of one club may visit and use the facilities of other clubs with shared objects or affiliations.

The authority for such activity is set out in Section 67 of the Licensing Act 2003. This Section employs the term 'associates' to describe a member of a club visiting a host club within the same reciprocal arrangement scheme and permits 'sales' to take place as opposed to the usual 'supply' when members make purchases. Visiting members enjoy the same facilities of membership other than voting rights.

Individual members and umbrella organisations both benefit from such a scheme. Members enjoy the freedom to visit other clubs while the objects of the umbrella organisation are strengthened by increased activity.

The Association of Conservative Club's 'Inter-Affiliation Ticket Scheme' is governed by the following Rules and Regulations–

## Rules governing the issue of Inter-Affiliation (IA) Tickets

• Inter-Affiliation (IA) Tickets can only be obtained by Inter-Affiliated clubs from the Secretary of the Association of Conservative Clubs (ACC). They are not transferable from club to club and can only be used by members of the club from which the tickets are issued. Secretaries, or others, breaking this rule render their club liable to immediate expulsion from the Association.

• Every IA Ticket must be signed by the member receiving it at the time of issue, in the presence of the Secretary, or the club steward (if so authorised by the committee). Every IA Ticket must also bear the signature of the Secretary of the club issuing it, and the number of every such ticket and the name of the member to whom it is issued, must be entered in a book kept for that purpose.

• An IA Ticket issued to a member who is subsequently suspended from his club is invalid and cannot be used during the time of such suspension (see Rule 6(b)). In the case of his expulsion, the ticket must be surrendered to the Secretary of the issuing club and is, ipso facto, cancelled permanently.

• The Secretary of any club, whose committee have cancelled, for any cause, an IA Ticket, shall forward the name of the member to whom the ticket was issued to the Secretary of the ACC.

Rules governing the admission of Inter-Affiliated Members to Clubs

- No holder of an IA Ticket shall be admitted into an Inter-Affiliated club until he has produced his own club ticket for the inspection of a club official, showing that he has paid his subscription at his own club for the whole time during which he is admitted to the club he visits.

- On every day upon which he visits the club, he must also sign his name, enter the name of his own club and the number of his IA Ticket in the ACC Inter-Affiliated Members' Book kept for that purpose in each Inter-Affiliated Club. In doing so, he is declaring that he has paid his subscription to his own club for the current period, is eligible for the privileges of Inter-Affiliation, and pledges himself to abide by rules and regulations of the club he is visiting.

- The signature of the Inter-Affiliated member in the above-mentioned book shall in every case be compared by the doorkeeper, or some other official, with the signature on the IA Ticket, before the holder shall be admitted.

- The club steward shall on no account serve an Inter-Affiliated member until he is satisfied that the above formalities have been complied with.

- Inter-Affiliated members visiting a club shall have the same privileges and rights, and be subject to the same rules and regulations as an ordinary member (except when special regulations have been made under Section 8), but shall not be supplied with excisable articles for consumption off the club premises, take books from the club, or attend or vote at meetings

- IA Tickets shall not give the right of entering or using a club to:

- A person who has been an unsuccessful candidate for admission to the said club.

- Any member of any club who is under suspension or expulsion from the said club. A suspended member shall deliver up his IA Ticket to the secretary of the issuing club, who shall retain it until the period of suspension has expired, when the ticket shall be returned to him. Should the holder fail to deliver up the ticket to the Secretary within three days of demand, it shall forthwith be cancelled, and the number of the ticket reported to the Secretary of the ACC.

- The holder of any IA Ticket which has been cancelled by the committee of the club issuing it, or to a suspended or expelled member.

- The holder of an IA Ticket issued by any club which has ceased to exist or is no longer affiliated to the ACC or of which he is no longer a member.

• Any club knowingly admitting a suspended or expelled member, whose IA Ticket is cancelled, shall be liable to immediate expulsion from the Association.

• The committee of every Inter-Affiliated club reserves to itself the right to make special regulations (subject to permission of the ACC Council) as to the admission of Inter-Affiliated members, in which case a copy of the same shall be exhibited on the club notice board. Such permission shall not be required for the exclusion of IA Ticket holders whose permanent habitation is within a radius of ten miles of the club premises. The holder of an IA Ticket is reminded that admission to an Inter-Affiliated club is an act of courtesy which can be withheld, in the interests of the club, on any occasion or in respect of any individual at the discretion of the club committee of any Inter-Affiliated club.

• A notice shall be posted in a conspicuous position in every Inter-Affiliated club prohibiting the sale of any excisable article to any person not being an ordinary or Inter-Affiliated member. Any infringement of this rule will render the club liable to immediate expulsion from the Association.

• All questions concerning the rights and obligations of Inter-Affiliation shall be referred to the Council of the Association, whose decision shall be final.

- The Association may make such further, or other, regulations as to Inter-Affiliation as they may consider in the interest of Inter-Affiliated clubs, and can decline to supply tickets to, or can cancel the Inter-Affiliation of, any club at any time, without assigning any reasons.

## The Equality Act 2010

The Equality Act 2010 amalgamated several previous Acts that had dealt separately with various forms of discrimination and created a new concept of 'protected characteristics'. It offers protection and legal remedies to people with 'protected characteristics' who have suffered discrimination, victimisation or harassment and effectively replaced previous legislation. There are nine protected characteristics, and these are:

1. Age,
2. Disability,
3. Gender reassignment,
4. Marriage and civil partnership,
5. Pregnancy and maternity,
6. Race,
7. Religion or belief,
8. Sex,
9. Sexual orientation.

There is no limit to the damages which may be awarded to an employee (or ex-employee or job applicant) who successfully claims unlawful discrimination at an employment tribunal. The awards do not just take into account the expected financial loss of the claimant but can also include compensation for injury to feelings.

### Types of discrimination

### Direct discrimination

This is where a condition or requirement is applied by the employer which may clearly be to the detriment of a particular group of people. The difference in treatment must be due to one of the factors which are prohibited by legislation. Merely treating people differently does not necessarily indicate discrimination although tribunals can infer this in the absence of a satisfactory explanation for the difference.

## Indirect discrimination

This is where a condition or requirement is applied by the employer which, whilst appearing to apply equally to all employees, is such that:

- The proportion of one particular group that can comply is considerably smaller than those of another group, and

- The employer cannot show that the requirement or condition is justifiable, and

- The individual affected suffers a detriment as a result of his/her inability to comply.

## Victimisation

This does not just mean singling someone out but relates to where one person has made a claim (or is thought to have done so) which is covered by the Equality Act and as a result has been treated less favourably. They may have initiated proceedings related to a discrimination claim or supported the claim of another person. The complainant would have to show that the reason for the less favourable treatment is because of the protected act, and not for some other unrelated reason.

**EXAMPLE**

An employee raises a grievance against his kitchen manager claiming that he is treated less favourably because he is gay. The grievance is resolved but the employee is prevented from attending a training programme, which he had previously been told he could go on and this limits the potential for promotion from commis chef to assistant head chef.

## Harassment

Harassment is defined as unwanted conduct which has "the purpose, intentionally or unintentionally, of violating dignity or which creates an intimidating, hostile, degrading, humiliating or offensive environment".

Harassment can be ongoing or can be a one-off serious act. In the case of third-party harassment, an employer will only be liable if the harassment has occurred on at least two previous occasions, knows that it has taken place and has not taken reasonable steps to prevent it happening again. Third- party harassment will apply to all protected characteristics except for pregnancy and maternity and marriage and civil partnership. It should also be noted that just as civil marriage rights have been extended to same sex partners, civil partnership rights have now been extended to opposite sex partners.

**EXAMPLE**

A 48-year-old male bar worker is frequently humiliated by the predominantly female and young workforce, through specific reference to his age and sex. He raises this with his club steward, who does nothing, and the hostilities continue. He could claim harassment based on age and sex.

## Government guidance on fair and equal procedures

Government guidance states that in relation to equality between the sexes all qualifying clubs should adopt fair and equal procedures for admitting people to membership, electing club officials and on voting rights.

## Government guidance on sex equality conditions

However, the government's guidance goes on to note that although equal treatment on the grounds of sex is important to society generally, it is not a licensing objective. The guidance therefore cautions licensing authorities not to impose conditions that interfere with arrangements for granting membership or voting within the club.

The government's guidance also comments that it would be inappropriate to apply one set of rules to qualifying clubs and another set of rules to clubs that do not engage in qualifying activities and do not therefore require club premises certificates. Licensing authorities should not therefore seek to challenge the bona fides of any qualifying club on these grounds.

## Disability Discrimination

The following is an extract from an article published by the Minister for Disabled People addressing how the previous Disability Discrimination Act affects Private Members' Clubs and the advice offered is still relevant today:

> *'... Many clubs have found that all they need to do is make small changes to open up their goods and services to a whole new clientele. In fact, if you are a small club with a limited budget, you will not be expected to finance unaffordable building works.*
>
> *You will be expected to keep the needs of your disabled customers in mind and you need to be clear that you cannot wait until a disabled person wants to use your club before making any necessary adjustments. "Nobody ever asked us" is not an acceptable excuse.*
>
> *For some clubs, making 'reasonable adjustments' could include providing members of staff with disability awareness training, which would help them recognise the different needs of disabled customers.*
>
> *Did you know that by standing still a partially sighted customer can make eye contact? Or that it is helpful to people with hearing impairments if background noise and music is kept to a minimum? Other adjustments could include keeping walkways clutter-free, which would make a difference to a whole range of customers including elderly people.*
>
> *Many of these are based on common sense. For instance, if the bar is too high for someone in a wheelchair you could offer to serve them at their table. Or, it may not be necessary to build a ramp to your premises; perhaps buying a portable one, at a much cheaper cost, will be all that is required.*
>
> *I know that many of you are probably already offering this kind of helpful service, but perhaps now is the time to stand back and look at other areas of your club where you could make further adjustments to further benefit disabled customers.*
>
> *There are no hard and fast rules. What is reasonable for one club may not be reasonable for another. It will depend on the circumstances of each case, such as the facilities on offer, the cost of the adjustment and the resources available.*

*You should also be aware that if you employ staff, you already have a responsibility to make adjustments for disabled employees and for any disabled person applying for a job.*

*You might want to ask disabled customers or local disability organisations for suggestions on how to improve accessibility for disabled people. I know they will be eager to help.*

*In many instances, the smallest changes can make all the difference. So, if you are interested in opening your doors to disabled people and boosting your bottom line, you do not automatically need a refit, just a rethink.'*

## Data Protection Act 2018

### Introduction

The Data Protection Act 2018 sets out how the UK Parliament will comply with EU-wide data protection regulations known as 'GDPR' – General Data Protection Regulations. The Data Protection Act 2018 will remain in force even though the UK has now left the European Union.

Below I have set out in a series of Questions and Answers how GDPR and the Data Protection Act 2018 applies to the operation of members' clubs.

Data Protection - what is it all about?

- Data protection is not a new concept. It has been in place for many decades in various legal forms.

- The primary piece of legislation that was in force before the 2018 Act was the Data Protection Act 1998.

- On 25 May 2018, our data protection law was upgraded and set out in the General Data Protection Regulation 'GDPR'.

- The GDPR puts more onerous obligations on organisation in being able to demonstrate compliance with the law. You can be audited by the Information Commissioner's Office, and in cases of serious non-compliance, fined with a monetary penalty up to £18 million.

It is vital to start from basics and to map your personal data. By this, we mean identifying:

- Where your organisation collects personal data

- How it processes that data; and

- What it is used for?

## What is a data controller?

You are a **data controller** if you say how and why personal data is processed.

## What is a data processor?

You are a **data processor** if you are the one processing the data on the data controller's behalf. Just because you are a data processor doesn't mean that you do not have data protection obligations. Under the GDPR data processors are subject to direct enforcement by the ICO and compensation claims by data subjects. Also, if you are a data controller you have additional responsibilities under the GDPR to make sure your contracts with data processors comply with the GDPR.

## What is personal data?

The GDPR are concerned with the protection of personal data. It is important to understand what that means. Personal data is:

- Any information relating to an identified or identifiable living individual

An identifiable living individual is:

A living individual who can be identified, directly or indirectly, in particular by reference to the following data:

- Names
- Addresses
- Email addresses
- Telephone numbers
- Online identifier
- Identification numbers
- Location information
- Opinions

I am secretary of a small members club. Will the GDPR apply to us?

Yes. The terms of the GDPR will apply to anyone processing personal data except for individuals processing personal data for personal or household activities. You should appoint a Data Controller for your club – probably the Club Secretary would be most suited to this role.

For this purpose, as stated above, personal data means any information relating to an identifiable person who can be directly or indirectly identified in particular by reference to an 'identifier'. Such identifiers could include:

- Someone's name,

- Identification number,

- Location data,

- Online identifier or to one or more factors specific to the physical, physiological, genetic, mental, economic, cultural, or social identity of that natural person.

The GDPR sets out several data protection principles which must always be adhered to if you process personal data. In the main these are the same as were found in the GDPR's predecessor, the Data Protection Directive. However, there are some new elements which may affect data use by clubs and societies, as set out below. The GDPR applies to both automated personal data and to manual filing systems where personal data is accessible according to specific criteria (e.g. alphabetically or chronologically ordered sets of manual records containing personal data). This means that for clubs or societies holding the names, contact details or other personal information about members, then yes, the GDPR will apply.

**Do we have to register with the Information Commissioners Office?**

You no longer have to notify the ICO as a data controller. However, if you are currently a not-for profit organisation you probably have not had to so far anyway. You will still need to register for use of CCTV.

**Do we have to change our membership application form?**

This will depend on what exactly is in your current membership form, but you should certainly review what is currently in there. The transparency principle in the GDPR means that you must communicate information clearly to members at the point at which you collect data, and your membership or website are the ideal places to do this.

The 'purpose limitation principle' means that personal data must be collected for specified, explicit and legitimate purposes and not further processed in a way incompatible with those purposes, so membership forms should only be collecting information that is necessary for the club or society's needs. For example, a person's name and contact details are likely to be required so that they are contactable, e.g., about club events and meetings, for membership renewals and if emergency contact details are required in case of an accident. However, a person's occupation, for example, may be irrelevant for your purposes and if so, it should not appear on membership forms.

Data must be processed:

- Lawfully,
- Fairly, and
- In a transparent manner.

This means that you must inform individuals about how and what you plan to use their data for at the point at which you collect it so your application form must clearly set out this information. There are various other pieces of information that you must tell them about including:

- How long you are planning on keeping or using it for, and
- Whether you plan to transfer it to anyone (for example to an affiliate for marketing purposes). This information can be communicated via a privacy notice, privacy policy or T&Cs which should appear on the membership form itself, and on your website it you have one.
- Personal data must be accurate and, where necessary, kept up to date.
- Inaccurate data must be erased or rectified without delay. Therefore, you should be ensuring that members' details which you store are up to date by contacting them and requesting them to confirm details.

To process data, data controllers must be able to point to their lawful basis for processing. There are six of these to choose from:

- Consent
- Contract
- Legal obligation
- Vital interests
- Public task, and
- Legitimate interests

Clubs and societies are most likely to find the following the most appropriate:

- Consent - where the individual has given clear consent for you to process their personal data for a specific purpose.
- Contract - where the processing is necessary for a contract you have

with the individual, or because they have asked you to take specific steps before entering into a contract, or

- Legitimate interests - the processing is necessary for your legitimate interests or the legitimate interests of a third party unless there is a good reason to protect the individual's personal data which overrides those legitimate interests.

Once you have established what your lawful basis will be, this should be communicated to members, most easily done by including this information in your privacy notice on your membership form and website.

## Do we have to update our website?

Transparency is key to the GDPR so you should make sure that individuals are aware of how you plan to use their personal data. If your club or society has a website you should make sure that your privacy policy or terms and conditions clearly set out everything to do with your data processing activities – your contact details, your lawful basis for processing, what you plan to use the data for, how it will be processed and how long it will be retained. It should also set out how they can contact you with any queries about the processing of their data and provide information about their individual rights.

If you use any third parties in relation to your website – e.g. website hosting/ marketing agents – they as data processors will also have obligations. As data controller you must ensure you have a contract in place with them and have GDPR compliance provisions in that contract

## Do we have to complete any other documentation?

The accountability principle under the GPDR means that you must be able to demonstrate compliance. In line with this, the GDPR contains explicit provisions that require you to maintain internal records of your processing activities. Among other things, records must be kept on processing purposes, categories of personal data, recipients of personal data, and retention.

However, there is a limited exemption from the documentation obligation for small and medium-sized organisations. If you employ fewer than 250 people, you need only document processing activities that:

- Are not occasional, e.g., are more than just a one-off occurrence or something you do rarely; or

- Are likely to result in a risk to the rights and freedoms of individuals, e.g., something that might be intrusive or adversely affect individuals; or

- Involve special category data or criminal conviction and offence data (as defined by Articles 9 and 10 of the GDPR).

## What happens if we lose any members information?

The GDPR introduces a new obligation on data controllers in the form of breach notification. This means that if there is a data breach and data is destroyed or lost, altered or disclosed or if there has been unauthorised access to such data which results in a risk to the rights and freedoms of the individuals involved, you as a data controller have an obligation to report this to the Information Commissioners Office (ICO) within 72 hours. If there is a high risk of adversely affecting individuals' rights and freedoms you must also inform the individuals themselves, without undue delay. This applies whether the breach is accidental or malicious and can be something as simple as sending personal data to an incorrect recipient or a computing device containing personal data being lost or stolen.

Therefore, when there has been a breach, you must establish the likelihood and severity of the resulting risk to individual's rights and freedoms. If a risk is likely, you must inform the ICO. If a risk is unlikely and only has the potential to be a small inconvenience (such as the loss of a small list of telephone numbers with no other identifying information included) – no reporting is required. When assessing whether it affects individual rights and freedoms, Recital 85 of the GDPR give the following guidance:

"A personal data breach may, if not addressed in an appropriate and timely manner, result in physical, material or non-material damage to natural persons such as loss of control over their personal data or limitation of their rights, discrimination, identity theft or fraud, financial loss, unauthorised reversal of pseudonymisation, damage to reputation, loss of confidentiality of personal data protected by professional secrecy or any other significant economic or social disadvantage to the natural person concerned."

This means that a breach with the risk of causing emotional distress, physical or material damage must be notified. You must also document any data breaches, whether notification is required, and staff or volunteers should be trained so that they know the appropriate procedures to follow in case of such a data breach.

## Can we still send emails to members?

You can still send emails to individuals but should be clear about what lawful basis you are using to do this. Note that if you are sending marketing emails, you may also have to comply with the Privacy and Electronic Communication Regulations (PECR). If you are simply communicating with individuals about scheduled club meetings and events, the PECR will not be relevant.

As explained above, all processing requires a lawful basis. These include valid consent and legitimate interest. Consent is currently perhaps the most frequently used basis for communications. Whilst consent can still be used, it now comes with various burdens attached. If you are relying on consent to use personal data, data subjects have a number of rights including the right to access the data (meaning that you must provide them with all data which you hold about them within strict timelines), the right to withdraw consent (meaning that you will have to stop using their data) and the right to data portability. Furthermore, GDPR sets a high standard for consent and for consent to be valid, the following must be considered:

- Consent must be feely given, specific, informed, and unambiguous.

- It requires a positive opt-in and pre-checked boxes are no longer allowed.

- If you are requesting consent from members, it must be clear, concise and be separate from other terms and conditions.

- If you need consent for different processing activities, consent must be obtained for each activity – blanket consent is no longer valid.

- Any third parties relying on the consent must be identified.

- Members must be informed of their right to withdraw consent and told how to do this.

- You must document all consents – who, when, how and what you told members.

- Make sure consents are up-to-date and refresh them if anything changes.

- Avoid making consent a pre-condition of a service.

**Should we use 'consent' or 'legitimate interest' as the basis for keeping data?**

Due to the individual rights attached to personal data obtained based on consent, an alternative legal basis may be more appropriate. Consent is only appropriate if your members are to have real choice and control over how you use their data.

Legitimate interests may in some cases be a more appropriate option for clubs and societies. It is the most flexible basis for data processing and will often apply where data is being used in a way that would be reasonably expected and which will have minimal privacy impact or where there is a compelling justification for processing. A club or society's legitimate interests may be to inform its members of meetings and events, or to contact the members to obtain membership renewals. In order to rely on this basis the processing in question must be necessary – if the processing would not be reasonably expected or would cause unjustified harm, the individual's interest will outweigh that of the club and the club could not rely on this legal basis.

Therefore, make sure you identify which legal basis you will be relying on and inform your members in your privacy policy so that they are clear about how and why you will be emailing them.

**What do we do with details of members who have left?**

Another data principle is that of *'Data Minimisation'*. Personal data must be adequate, relevant, and limited to that necessary in relation to the purposes for which they are processed. Furthermore, the GDPR imposes a storage limitation requirement, meaning that personal data can be kept for no longer than necessary for the purpose for which it is processed. This data retention limit means that you must only keep data of members for as long as you need it for their membership. You should therefore ensure that you remove from your files or database information relating to people that are no longer members of the club. This does not prevent you from holding a database of lapsed members, but the timeframe for holding that information must be limited.

Is a locked filing cabinet or password protected database containing members' information sufficiently secure for the purposes of the GDPR?

Personal data must be processed in a manner that ensures appropriate security of the personal data. This includes protection against unauthorised or unlawful processing and against accidental loss, destruction, or damage, using appropriate technical or organisational measures. The security measures in place will depend on the data controller and what type and volume of personal data is being processed. The level of security must be appropriate to the risk posed to the personal data being processed. A locked filing cabinet or password protected database (with the password only known to those who require access e.g., the club secretary) may well be appropriate security for a small, local club holding only members names

113

and contact details but not for a large organisation holding larger volumes and more complex personal data who will require much more advanced security measures to ensure compliance. Even so, if a locked filing cabinet is used, make sure it is in a secure room, always locked and that the key is kept secure. Password protected systems should be backed up regularly.

If you are also collecting bank details from members for payment, keep these in a separate, secure location.

Importantly, staff or volunteers should be aware of the GDPR security requirements and be trained on breach notification procedures.

Can individuals ask to see the information we hold about them?

Yes. Under the GDPR, individuals have:

- The right to obtain confirmation that you are processing their personal data and

- The right of access to the personal data. So, you must respond to them without delay and always within one month.

- This must be done free of charge unless an individual repeatedly and excessively requests information in which case a reasonable fee may be imposed taking account of the administrative costs involved.

- Before responding to such a request, ensure you verify the identity of the person making the request using reasonable means.

**What if we process children's information?**

There are additional safeguards in place for children's personal data. If you process children's data, you must ensure that your privacy policy is written in plain, simple English. Privacy notices should be very clear for children so that they are able to understand what will happen to their personal data, and what rights they have.

Note that if you are relying on consent as your lawful basis for processing personal data, when offering an online service directly to a child, only children aged 13 or over are able provide their own consent. If they are younger you must obtain consent from the parent or guardian.

If you are relying upon the 'legitimate interests' basis you must take responsibility for identifying the risks and consequences of the processing and put age appropriate safeguards in place.

## Action Plan

1. Map out the journey that personal data takes as it passes through your club. What information do you currently collect? Do you need all this information? What are individuals told at the point of collection? On what legal basis are you collecting it? What do you do with it? How is it secured? How long do you hold it for?

2. Make sure your privacy policies are up to date so that people are informed about your lawful basis for processing, who you are, why you are collecting their data, how you plan to use it and how long you will hold it for.

3. Ensure that relevant staff or volunteers are aware of and adequately trained on the GDPR requirements and know who to contact in case of data access requests or breaches.

Make sure you have appropriate and up–to-date data policies and procedures in place to help staff and volunteers understand data protection issues and solutions.

Detailed GDPR advice documents and templates can be accessed free for Association of Conservative Club members on our website at: https://www.toryclubs.co.uk/gdpr-documents-pack/ For non-ACC members, please contact our office by email on: assistance@toryclubs.co.uk or telephone us on: 0207 222 0868.

## Pubwatch

Clubs often ask the question: 'Is it lawful for a club to join a Pubwatch Scheme?' The simple answer to this question is, 'Yes, it is.' However, the wider answer to this question is a little more complex.

Under the Licensed Premises (Exclusion of Certain Persons) Act 1980, courts have the power to ban the persons convicted of an offence on licensed premises in which violence was used or threatened. They may make an order excluding the convicted persons from licensed premises for a period of between three months and two years. The order may apply to the premises where the offence was committed or to any other specified licensed premises. If a person breaks an order, a further penalty of a fine or imprisonment may be imposed. It should be noted that the order applies to licensed premises and, therefore, is not extended to clubs.

In various parts of the country, police authorities have been active in setting up Pubwatch schemes. Where an individual is reported to have been violent on licensed premises, his name is circulated to all members of the scheme. He is then banned from all the premises of scheme members. It is possible, therefore, for a ban to be imposed, although there has been no actual conviction.

The significance of Pubwatch schemes for clubs is that in some areas where Private Members' Clubs have been invited to join and to observe the ban on named individuals. While this may be a contribution to discouraging violence among the drinking fraternity, membership of a Pubwatch scheme could produce problems for clubs.

The rules adopted by most clubs lay down their own course of action for the disciplinary treatment of club members and provide the committee with the authority to reprimand, suspend or expel any member who infringes the rules or any member whose conduct in or out of the club is prejudicial to the club's interest. Such rules will always provide that members shall not be disciplined without first being given a full opportunity to defend themselves before the committee.

It must be appreciated that a club's rules provide members with certain rights. These rights cannot be taken away by the imposition of an automatic suspension or expulsion required by a club's membership of a Pubwatch scheme. If an attempt were made to do so, a member would almost certainly win an appeal to arbitration. Therefore, membership of a Pubwatch scheme may raise some possible conflict with a club's rules.

There are certain benefits for clubs joining Pubwatch schemes, but clubs must do so with the clear understanding that they cannot subscribe to every aspect of a scheme's requirements. For example, some schemes always require participating pubs and clubs to permit police access to the premises. Registered clubs are established as private places and in normal circumstances a police officer does not have access to a club's premises without a warrant. Such a condition in joining a Pubwatch scheme should therefore be rejected.

If a Pubwatch scheme is operating in your area, then find out whether there is any value in your club becoming involved but bear in mind the fact that clubs are, by their very nature, independent.

### Liability for Lost or Stolen Property

The problem of a member's lost or stolen property is one which is, unfortunately, experienced by most clubs at some time and the advice given depends on the actual circumstances of each individual case. However, whatever circumstances, the question of bailment applies. Bailment is the delivery of goods by one person, called the bailer, to another person, called the bailee.

Halsbury's Laws of England defines bailment as: 'a delivery of personal chattels in trust on a contract, express or implied, that the trust shall be duly executed and the chattels redelivered in either their original or an altered form, as soon as the time, or use for, or condition on which they were bailed, shall have elapsed or been performed.'

In most cases, members simply leave their personal belongings in the club and return to find them missing. If, however, a club is to attract any liability for the lost or stolen property of a member or guest, then it would be as a gratuitous bailee. To this end, the person claiming a loss would have to show that there had been an actual delivery and acceptance of their property by the club before there could be any obligation on the club as bailee.

The important factor would be that the club accepted the property and became, in some degree, responsible for it whilst it remained on the club premises. For example, if a club merely provides the facilities of a coat rack and there is no employee of the club who takes proper custody of garments left there, then a person who loses property would be unable to sustain a good claim against the club for the loss.

During the nineteenth century, a bailment case was heard. In this case, a man entered a restaurant to dine and, without being asked, a waiter helped him to take off his coat and hung it on a hook behind him whilst he was dining. The man got up to find that the coat had been stolen. The fact that the waiter took the coat is strong evidence that the restaurant became a bailee of the coat, and the man was successful in his claim.

There are, obviously, several distinguishing features between this reported case and the example of the club providing a coat rack. Clubs are well advised to post a notice in the club indicating that the club accepts no responsibility for the loss of property of any member or any other persons on the club premises. A suitable notice would read: "The club accepts no responsibility for loss or damage to personal property, however sustained, on the premises of the club."

## Noise Pollution

Clubs always try to be good neighbours to people who live nearby but occasionally even the best regulated clubs may do something that will cause a complaint. Often this concerns noise, possibly from enthusiastic entertainers whose music can be heard outside the club or from members leaving the premises inconsiderately. Many clubs put up notices urging members to be careful not to upset the neighbours with excessive noise because complaints can cause ill-feeling, trouble and can cost money.

Noise is classed as a 'statutory nuisance' under the Environmental Health Act 1990 and if a complaint is made and ignored, the club could find itself in court and facing a heavy fine. Sensible clubs would take steps to deal with the situation before a complaint reaches this stage, but it is essential to do something once there is the suggestion that noise is causing a problem.

There are various stages that must take place before a noise nuisance case gets to court. A person with a complaint would take it to their local authority who would usually write to the club pointing out that there has been a complaint. Under no circumstances should such a letter be ignored in the hope that the complaint will go away; it will not. The club should take steps to deal with the alleged nuisance and then seek advice before attempting to reply. If the situation is still not resolved, the local authority would then issue an 'abatement notice'. At this stage, the club must seek legal advice. Doing nothing is not an option. Club officers should bear in mind that if a complaint about noise does reach court, and is proved, the fine can amount to a massive £20,000.

**Playing copyright music (recorded or live) in your club**

If you allow the playing of music, either live or recorded, by any means in your club then you are playing music whose copyright is owned by others. You therefore require a copyright permission for the performance of that music to be lawful. In practice this means paying a licence fee to two copyright organisations – Phonographic Performance Limited (PPL) and the Performing Rights Society (PRS). PPL acts on behalf of record companies and performers and PRS acts on behalf of songwriters, composers, and publishers.

Previously, businesses and organisations had to obtain separate music licences from PPL and PRS for Music for the playing or performance of copyright music. However, these two organisations have now come together to form PPL PRS Ltd and launch 'The Music Licence'. What does this mean?

The Music Licence allows you to legally play or perform copyright music for employees or customers in your club through the radio, TV, other digital devices, and live performances. **So, two separate licences are no longer required: One contact. One invoice. One licence.**

How it works

Licence fees from UK businesses and organisations are collected on behalf of their parent companies, PPL and PRS for Music.

PPL then distributes these music licence fees for the use of recorded music on behalf of record companies and performers, while PRS for Music distributes music licence fees for the use of musical compositions and lyrics on behalf of songwriters, composers, and publishers.

This ensures that the people who create music receive payment for the use of their copyright material and artistic creations.

The cost of The Music Licence depends on several factors, including your type of venue and how you use music. For more information, contact PPL PRS Limited.

## Children's Parties and Disclosure and Barring Checks

Employers can apply to check the criminal record of someone applying for a role. This is known as getting a Disclosure and Barring Service (DBS) check. You can request a more detailed check for certain roles, for example in healthcare or childcare.

DBS checks apply in England and Wales, there are different rules for getting a criminal record check in Scotland and Northern Ireland.

The Disclosure and Barring Service (DBS) is an Executive Agency of the Home Office and was set up to help organisations make safer recruitment decisions. Whether it is necessary to obtain a DBS check for persons supervising a children's party in a club will vary depending upon who the supervisors are and what their role is.

If the supervisors are simply parents of the children in question, then no checks will be required for a 'one off' event such as this. This will also apply if volunteers are used and it will ultimately be up to the organiser of the event to be satisfied that they are all suitable to work with children. A lack of prescribed legislation emphasises that it will be at the organiser's discretion; if they feel further checks on an individual are necessary then they should not hesitate in requiring them.

If supervisors are hired and they host this type of event for a living, then they will have already had to been required to disclose any convictions when applying for a job that involves working with children. All organisations that provide these services will require a DBS check for all employees before they can work. It is always a good idea to request confirmation that this is the case.

Other points to be aware of include ensuring that the building itself is suitable for the type of activity, that the numbers do not exceed the club's capacity and that there are suitable protocols in place for first aid emergencies etc.

Clubs that wish to carry out criminal records checks on members of staff must use a Registered Organisation. These are umbrella bodies that carry out large numbers of criminality checks for a variety of organisations and purposes. It is not possible to become a Registered Organisation unless you are submitting a minimum of 100 DBS checks per year.

## Types of check

You can request:

- A basic check, which shows unspent convictions and conditional cautions

- A standard check, which shows spent and unspent convictions, cautions, reprimands, and final warnings

- An enhanced check, which shows the same as a standard check plus any information held by local police that is considered relevant to the role

- An enhanced check with barred lists, which shows the same as an enhanced check plus whether the applicant is on the list of people barred from doing the role

  If you carry out criminal records checks, you must have a policy on employing ex-offenders and show it to any applicant who asks for it.

## DBS code of practice

Registered Bodies must:

- Use all reasonable endeavours to ensure that they only submit criminal records check applications in accordance with the legislative provisions which provide eligibility criteria for relevant positions or employment.

- Ensure that before allowing a DBS check application to be submitted they have assessed the role to be eligible under current legislation, correctly applied the right level of check, and correctly requested the appropriate barring list information.

- Ensure they are legally entitled to request any DBS product being applied for.

As a small employer using a Registered Organisation acting as an umbrella body, the code directly applies to the Registered Organisation, and they will rely on you to provide them with accurate information to comply with their obligations.

## Smoking Ban

Smoking is no longer permitted in clubs since the introduction of the Smoking Ban. Workplace smoking bans were also implemented to prevent employees smoking at work.

Clubs must display at least one A5 'No Smoking' sign at every entrance and exit to the club and fines will be incurred for not displaying these signs. There will be an evaluation in future to decide whether it will be necessary to continue to display them.

An individual smoking within a club will initially receive a fixed penalty of £50. If the same individual repeats the offence, then fines will increase to £200. If a club fails to prevent a member from smoking within the club premises, then the club can be fined £2,500.

A club may be able to show that action was taken to prevent a member from smoking by–

- Requesting the individual to put the cigarette out

- Having witnesses to this request

- Entering details in club records to this effect

If the club can show they did everything possible to prevent smoking they will probably escape a fine.

Interestingly, clubs are still able to sell cigarettes and the taking of snuff continues to be permitted on club premises.

### 'Substantially Enclosed'

If a club can provide comfortable outdoor facilities for smokers then it is likely to retain its patronage and may, in fact, increase custom from other establishments which have no such facilities. This scenario can, of course, work the other way.

The Health Act 2006 permits smoking to take place in facilities that are largely open to the air and that do not fall within the meaning under the Act of being 'substantially enclosed'.

The Smoke-free (Premises and Enforcement) Regulations 2006 provide the meaning of 'substantially enclosed' premises–

*'Premises are deemed substantially enclosed if they have a ceiling or roof, but there is an opening in walls, or an aggregate area of openings in the walls, which is less than half of the area of the walls, including other structures that serve the purpose of walls and constitute the perimeter of the premises.*

*In determining the area of an opening (or an aggregate area of openings) no account is to be taken of openings in which there are doors, windows or other fittings that can be opened or shut.*

*A roof includes any fixed or moveable structure or device which is capable of covering all or part of the premises as a roof including, for example, a canvas awning.'*

In other words, a structure with a roof and at least three open sides would be acceptable. This is sometimes referred to as the '50% Rule.' Many companies have sprung up to provide awnings and canopies to meet this new demand. However, this is not a case of buying a bit of garden furniture. It is an important investment which needs to be considered. In many cases, planning permission may be required.

## Equipment Leasing

There are many companies in existence who are in the business of providing equipment, ranging from door entry systems and tills to CCTV cameras, screens and projectors and even major air conditioning work to clubs on lease arrangements.

The information supplied by these companies often looks attractive and the sales personnel employed are mostly smart and personable. However, the fact is that most offers, whilst at a glance might appear good value, ultimately involve complex leasing contracts which run for many years and sometimes incorporate automatic renewable terms in the event of cancellation notices not being provided by clubs within a specified time slot.

Leasing works on a hire purchase system and equipment will never ultimately belong to the club. In almost every case, companies selling the equipment use a separate finance company which owns the equipment and it is this finance company which a club will have to deal with if there are problems with either the equipment or the lease. Therefore when problems occur, the companies which sell the equipment to clubs no longer wish to be involved and clubs are left to defend themselves against finance companies which are always quick to threaten legal action in an aggressive manner, introducing additional financial penalties which add further financial costs and often anxiety to club officers.

Some clubs have ended up paying in the region of £23,000 for a simple door entry system and in one case a club calculated that £48,000 had been spent over ten years on a door entry system which was no longer being used. In each case, the leasing contracts were legally binding and left no escape route for the clubs concerned.

I strongly advise clubs not to enter into leasing arrangements for such equipment, however plausible the offers may appear to be. Glossy brochures and smart-talking salesmen cannot hide the fact that clubs would be better off buying the advertised equipment outright (with perhaps an additional simple maintenance agreement) or borrowing the money from a bank to purchase outright what is required.

All clubs with such agreements in place should re-examine the contracts they have entered into and make careful notes as to when cancellation notices should be made. Also avoid agreeing to offers of upgrading lease equipment already in place which invariably create new contract terms.

## Foreign Supplied Television

Clubs risk prosecution for using foreign decoder cards to show foreign supplied television broadcast from overseas, which could result in a big fine and a hefty bill of costs. This includes Premier League football matches.

The Media Protection Services (MPS) safeguards the rights of the FA Premier League. MPS admits that there is a vast amount of misinformation circulated on the internet by the importers of and dealers in decoder cards which are backed by a 'handful of solicitors.'

MPS is committed to stopping the illegal commercial broadcasting of these matches in pubs and clubs. Any licensee or club Secretary who appears to be using a foreign decoder card is sent a legal notice warning of the criminal offence they are committing if they use such a card.

In the legal notice, issued on behalf of the Premier League and BskyB, it is stated clearly that 'no individual or company is authorised to sell you a system or decoder card issued by an overseas broadcaster to enable you to receive transmissions neither is any fee paid to such an individual or company an 'applicable fee' that enables you to receive the transmissions without a BSkyB commercial agreement.' The legal notice also advises disregarding any representation made by suppliers of foreign decoder cards who offer a valid subscription for receipt of signals from an overseas broadcaster. If the notice is ignored, then an undercover visit will be paid to the premises and prosecution of the responsible person is likely to be set in train.

The dealers of foreign decoder cards try to argue that 'European directives' make it legally possible to use foreign decoder cards. This is not so and there is no directive which takes away the power of copyright owners to protect their copyright under British Law. They also contend that overseas broadcasters have bought 'rights' to show Premiership games and purchase of the decoder cards entitles people to show the matches. The only UK company assigned rights by the copyright owner (Premier League Ltd.) is BSkyB. Dealers of foreign decoder cards also claim that the Department of Culture Media and Sport has issued a letter confirming that the use of foreign cards in the UK is legal. This is not the case and is based on a letter from the DCMS, which accepted that it was not illegal to bring cards into the country but which went on to make it clear that use of the cards was an infringement of copyright and a criminal offence. It also emphasised that BSkyB was the only copyright holder.

Overseas broadcasters, licensed by the FA Premier League to receive matches in their territory, have confirmed that decoder cards that they issue remain their property and are authorised for use in their territory. They also confirm it is not possible to buy a subscription direct from an overseas broadcaster to receive Premiership matches in the UK.

I should point out that I do not act for, or support, BSkyB. In my opinion, Sky's charges to clubs are too high and have been so for some time. It is perhaps because of these high charges that dealers have been able to convince so many outlets to broadcast foreign supplied TV. I have had meetings with BSkyB and informed them that their charges are too high and that they would sign up many more clubs if their charges were reduced, but this has had no effect.

**Men Only/Lady Members**

A detailed description of a club's responsibilities under the Equality Act 2010 was given earlier in this book. This legislation does not require clubs which are already established with single sex membership to open their membership to the opposite sex. Gender is not a protected characteristic under the Equality Act 2010, but sex and gender reassignment are. Clubs which are therefore men only or women only, and which do not elect women or men to non-voting membership are not required to change.

## General

### Accidents in Clubs

The liability of a club to pay compensation for injury or damage to a member's or visitor's person or property while on the premises depends on the circumstances. A claim by any person against a club for damages sustained as a result of an accident occurring on the premises would not be successful unless the claimant could prove that the accident was caused by the fault or negligence of any club official or employee. A non-member such as a visitor would certainly have a right of action against the club, but whether a member could in such circumstances sue his own club, would depend upon the facts. Club committees are advised in the interests of themselves, members, members' guests, and visitors, to insure against such accidents.

### Correspondence

No club official or employee has any right to open correspondence addressed to the Secretary. There may be certain occasions whereby a special reason, such as a question of urgency, would mean that such an act would not be deemed an offence. But any person opening a letter not intended for him wilfully and with malicious intent, or who prevents or impedes its due delivery to the addressee, is liable to prosecution under the Post Office Act 1953.

### Food Safety Act 1990

Under the Act and associated Regulations, clubs serving food or drink must register with their local authority. It is an offence to supply contaminated or unfit food. Authorised food officers can enter premises without notice to inspect food and catering arrangements, seize suspect items, and in bad cases close premises. It is also an offence to obstruct a food officer or to withhold information or assistance without reasonable cause. There are strict temperature limits for keeping and storing many foodstuffs. A defence of 'due diligence' in taking precautions is available, and staff must be given enough training for their tasks. Penalties for serious offences are very heavy.

### Smuggled Goods

There has been an increase of smuggled alcohol and cigarettes into the UK and this has become a problem for clubs. Section 144 of the Licensing Act 2003 provides that any officer or member of a club who fails to prevent smuggled goods from being kept on club premises may be charged with an offence. Clubs should ensure that such goods are not purchased or kept on the premises of the club.

## 10.0    MEETINGS

### Club Meetings: Points of Procedure

Club meetings are of two kinds:

1. General Meetings, to which all members of the club are summoned, and

2. Committee Meetings, which only duly appointed members of the committee are eligible to attend.

The principal General Meeting each year is the Annual General Meeting, which is held at the stated time and for stated purposes (the transaction of business) as laid down in the rules. Any other General Meeting is a Special General Meeting convened for a special reason as defined in the rules.

### General Meeting

### Notice

Every meeting must be properly summoned by the Secretary, either by sending a notice to all members entitled to attend or by display of announcement on the notice board. Length of notice should be stated in the rules.

### Agenda

Every member should receive an agenda. This is frequently incorporated with the notice of the meeting. It should be concise and clearly set out. When a motion has been tabled, exact wording should be given. 'Any other business' should not appear on the agenda for a General Meeting.

### Quorum

There must be a quorum present at a meeting to enable business to be transacted. The number should be laid down in the rules. If a quorum is not present within a reasonable time of the hour appointed for the meeting, the meeting is automatically adjourned. No quorum is required for an AGM unless the rules state otherwise.

### Meeting Chairman

The President should preside *ex officio*; in his absence the Chairman presides and failing him the Vice-Chairman. If neither is present, the meeting elects its own Chairman. In such cases the Secretary or convener of the meeting should ask for nominations. No seconder is needed. If more than one nomination is received, the names should be put in alphabetical order and the person receiving the highest number of votes takes the Chair at once.

The primary duty of a Chairman is to decide who is entitled to address the meeting, and to maintain order. He must not allow any discussion unless it bears directly on the subject under discussion. He should allow no member to speak when the mover of a motion or amendment has resumed his seat unless such member rises to second the resolution or amendment under discussion. The Chairman's decision on all points of order is final. If his directions are disobeyed, he should declare the meeting adjourned, and quit the Chair.

## Validity of Meeting

The first business of the Chairman is to call on the Secretary to read the notice summoning the meeting or alternatively to ask if it shall 'be taken as read' by consent.

## Confirmation of Minutes

The Chairman should next call upon the Secretary to read the Minutes of the previous meeting. After they have been read and before any question or discussion is allowed, the Chairman must ask for the motion: That the Minutes are confirmed as a true record of the previous meeting. Once this has been duly moved, seconded, and agreed, the Chairman signs the Minutes close to the last line, thereby preventing subsequent additions. No one should be allowed to discuss the business recorded in the previous Minutes; the only matter on which discussion can take place is whether they are an accurate report of the previous meeting. Questions can now be asked to ascertain whether the resolutions recorded in the minutes have been carried out and any motion not hostile to, or varying such resolutions, may be accepted by the Chairman. If anyone desires to amend or rescind any of the resolutions, due notice must be given for inclusion in the agenda for the next meeting.

## Business for which the Meeting was Convened

This must be transacted in the order in which it appears on the agenda. The order cannot be changed except with the consent of a three-quarters majority of the members voting.

## Motions

A motion should be moved by the person named on the agenda, unless the meeting agrees to some other person moving it. No discussion on any motion should be permitted until it has been seconded. If the motion is not seconded it lapses, and the Chairman should proceed to the next business. A motion may be withdrawn by the proposer either before or during discussion, with the permission of the seconder and of the meeting. Such a withdrawal cannot take place after the motion has been voted on.

## Amendments

An amendment is a proposal to alter the wording of a motion. More than one amendment may be put forward on any one motion, but only one may be discussed at a time. An amendment must have a bearing on the subject of the motion; it should not be a direct negative, since it is open to anyone who is totally opposed to the motion to speak and vote against it. Like a motion, an amendment must be proposed and seconded before it can be discussed. The withdrawal of an amendment is carried out in the same way as that of a motion.

## Voting

After an amendment has been discussed, the Chairman should read out the motion and the amendment. He should ask 'those in favour' of the amendment to show hands and then 'those against.' If an amendment is carried, it becomes the 'substantive motion,' which means it replaces the motion in its original form and becomes the subject before the meeting for further discussion and amendment. At the close of the debate the motion is put to the vote, either in its original form or as amended.

## Preparing for an AGM

An AGM is held to transact certain business: the report on the ballot for officers and committee (unless they are elected at the AGM itself); the report on the accounts; the adoption of the accounts, as audited; and other reports as required by a club's own rules.

Firstly, it is essential for the AGM to be properly summoned. This usually involves a notice being placed on the club notice board announcing the date and time of the meeting and requesting motions to be submitted to the Secretary by a certain date.

The rules of most clubs provide that a notice of the AGM shall be exhibited at least twenty-one days before the date of the meeting; and the notice of any motion must be submitted within ten days following the posting of the notice. Rules can also say that the agenda must be posted for a specified number of days before the date of the meeting.

Before the meeting it is essential for whoever is taking the Chair–Club President or Chairman depending on the club's rules–to undertake a careful study of the agenda. This will mean he can conduct the business effectively and spot any difficult matters that might arise. Preparation is crucial to the success of the meeting.

When the meeting starts, the Chairman should satisfy himself that the requisite quorum is present. Most club rules require a quorum. This is to prevent a small, poorly attended meeting making decisions which affect the whole club.

The meeting must proceed with each item of business taken in the order in which it appears on the agenda. A normal agenda begins with confirmation of the minutes of the previous AGM, any business arising from them, then the Treasurer's report on the accounts, the election of officers, and so on.

The presiding officer, mindful of the need for a well-ordered, good tempered and constructive meeting, must see that the agenda is followed strictly. Speakers should stand when called by the chairman and, to preserve order, only one person should be on their feet at the same time. When the Chairman rises any other speaker should sit down and this should be insisted upon. Unless this is done, a meeting can degenerate into disarray and chaos.

A proposal for discussion is a 'motion' and when it is accepted it becomes a 'resolution'. Before discussion begins, a motion must be proposed and seconded. A motion that is proposed, but finds no seconder, lapses, and the meeting proceeds to next business. When a motion is proposed and seconded it is open for discussion. No speaker should be allowed to address the meeting more than once on each motion, except for the proposer, who may reply to the debate. A motion may be ultra vires–that is, outside the scope of the meeting–and should immediately be ruled out of order by the chairman.

An amendment is a proposal to alter the wording of a motion and may be moved at any time during the discussion of the original motion. Special care must be taken over this if the meeting is not to be allowed to become confused. The proposal requires a proposer and seconder before it can be considered by the meeting. The chairman should present an amendment to the meeting, once it has been properly proposed and seconded, in terms such as: 'To the motion before the meeting the following amendment has been duly proposed and seconded, that...' The wording of the amendment then follows, and the immediate discussion must be confined to the subject of the amendment. Some bodies permit amendments to be moved to amendments, but it is NOT recommended for clubs. If it is allowed it can prolong discussion and make for a complicated passage of business. In practice the proposer of the main amendment may incorporate in it what he considers best in suggestions for further amendments, if he accepts, they will improve his proposal. No amendment may be a direct negative to the main motion for this would merely duplicate the need to vote on a particular proposition. An amendment must be disposed of before the meeting can proceed to a further amendment. If an amendment is accepted it becomes part of the original motion; it is then called the substantive motion. Further amendments may be considered in turn until all have been dealt with. Then, discussions may continue on the substantive motion until it is put to the vote. Before the vote on each amendment the chairman should repeat its wording so that there is a clear understanding of the matter on which a vote is being taken.

Similarly, the substantive motion should be read out again before the vote. When those 'for' and 'against' in each vote have been counted, the chairman should announce the result. If many people are voting, the President should appoint two 'tellers' to count the votes. The tellers should both count the 'yes' and 'no' votes. If there is any disagreement the vote MUST be taken again. When an issue is controversial a close vote may be disputed so it is useful to be prepared for a written vote.

One further possible motion is 'That this meeting do now adjourn.' This takes precedence over all other business and may be moved at any time during a meeting. The Chairman should not accept such a motion if he thinks it is being moved with the intention of disrupting the meeting. The decision is made on the vote of the meeting, on a motion proposed and seconded, and without lengthy discussion. Amendments are possible but only to set, limit or extend the period of the adjournment.

The correct conduct of a meeting is not an easy skill to master, but many difficulties can be avoided if the presiding officer follows the procedures set out here. However, even this will not guarantee that meetings are without problems. Some issues will so divide the membership that heated, and sometimes irresolvable, exchanges are inevitable. Nevertheless, a basic knowledge of tried, and accepted, procedures will help ensure that most meetings are managed efficiently.

## Committee Meetings

The rules of procedure relating to the conduct of committee meetings are the same as at General and Special General Meetings with the following exceptions–

- It is not necessary that the Chairman be addressed by members standing

- The general rule that only one speech may be made by the same member on the same question, may, at the discretion of the Chairman, be suspended

- The meeting can, at the discretion of the Chairman, transact business which is not specified on the agenda

Every committee member has the right to be informed of the time and place of a meeting of the committee. If this is not done, a meeting of only a few members has no power to make decisions.

When vacancies occur on committees, they should be filled as soon as possible, and it is desirable that the rules provide for this to be done. Any person may be nominated for any number of posts in a club. Sometimes, the rules state that no one shall be nominated for more than one post at a time. If a person is already the holder of one, this does not preclude his name from being put forward for another. If he is elected to the latter post, he may then vacate his existing position. If he is unsuccessful, he simply retains his existing position.

Trustees are normally able to be elected to members of committees and can then vote and speak in the usual way. It is possible, however, for the rules to limit such a right.

On occasion, there are issues which are of considerable immediate concern to all the membership. Indeed, some point or other may have been referred from a General Meeting to the Committee for special consideration. In such cases, the committee should authorise the Secretary to arrange for the necessary information to be transmitted to the membership, e.g., by a report at a General Meeting, or by circulation of such a report.

## A Code of Standing Orders for Committees

- In the absence of the Chairman, a committee may proceed to business after electing a temporary Chairman

- The first business at all ordinary meetings shall be the approval of past ordinary Minutes; the only permissible discussion shall be the accuracy of the record

- Objections must be moved, seconded, and voted upon

- The Chairman shall maintain order and keep all 'points of order' in accordance with this code: decide priority of speeches according to the order in which a member 'catches his eye' and ask for the terms of a motion or amendment before a speech is delivered, if the Chairman thinks fit

- In the case of disorder arising, the Chairman shall have power to adjourn the meeting to a time fixed by the Chairman, and when the Chairman leaves the chair all business shall be terminated

- In the case of equality of votes, the Chairman shall have a second or casting vote at committee meetings only

- Notice must be given at least five days before an ordinary meeting of any motions to be proposed other than those which arise directly from the subject under discussion

- Alterations or rescindments of existing minutes or resolutions must be by notice at the previous ordinary meeting and motion proposed, seconded, and carried

- Motions and amendments must not be withdrawn or essentially altered after they have been seconded without permission of the meeting

- The motion 'to pass to the next business' shall always have priority over other amendments, and if this is carried the meeting shall at once proceed to the consideration of the next business

- The mover of an original resolution shall have the right of reply but must not introduce new matter

- If a member rises to 'a point of order' the member must specify the rule in the code which he thinks is being violated, and the member who was in possession of the meeting shall wait until the point of order has been discussed and settled

- Only the Chairman can rule on a point of order; the speaker shall then continue the speech subject to the ruling which has been given

- Discussion shall cease if the motion that 'the question be now put' is carried by a majority, the mover of an original motion having been first heard in reply

- At an adjourned debate, the mover of the adjournment shall be first heard

- The Chairman of a committee shall have power to summon special meetings for urgent business or at the written requisition of a majority of the members of such committee, the special business to be placed on the notice calling the same

- No minutes of ordinary meetings will be read at special meetings

- Programme of business for all meetings shall be circulated three days before the meeting

- Sub-committees must report to the general committee before acting upon their resolutions unless they have been given executive powers

- At the first meeting of a sub-committee the Chairman of such committee shall be appointed and the number of members necessary to form a quorum shall be decided upon

- The Chairman of the general committee shall have the right to attend and vote at all sub-committees

These standing orders can only be suspended by a majority of the members present.

## Confidentiality

The confidentiality of committee meetings is paramount to the effective management of a club. Discussion in committee should remain confidential between committee members.

The Minutes of committee meetings should merely record the motions and amendments and decisions which are agreed and, again, remain confidential. This does not mean that there are never circumstances in which the membership ought to be informed of what takes place during committee meetings.

In all clubs there are issues which are of immediate concern to all the membership. The committee may have discussed some matter referred to it by a general meeting for consideration. In such cases, the Secretary should arrange for a suitable notice to be posted on the club notice board.

The general membership does not have a right to inspect the committee's Minutes.

However, a club's auditors will have a right to inspect the committee's Minutes to confirm that certain transactions have been authorised.

In addition, clubs registered under the Friendly Societies Act are obliged to permit members to examine all books, including all Minute books, at any reasonable time. This is a good reason why the Minutes should read like a telegram and not like a social history.

There are, however, few clubs registered as Friendly Societies. Such clubs are different from those registered under the Industrial and Provident Societies Act.

No member of the committee is entitled to inform anyone of the proceedings and deliberations of the committee. If a club is to be served well, then it is essential that the committee should be free to conduct their affairs in a frank and open way. Surely, few people would serve on committees if they knew that their views were repeated outside the confines of the committee room and, as is so often the case, misinterpreted by being taken out of context and made to appear contrary to the original intentions.

Committees are therefore entitled to insist on the confidentiality of their proceedings and the right of quasi privilege in the conduct of the affairs of the club while, at the same time, keeping the members informed of matters that affect them generally, but not in respect to individual members.

Proceedings in committee are not privileged, but qualified privilege may apply where the person who makes the communication has an interest or duty, legal or moral or social, to make it to a person, or persons, having a corresponding interest or duty to receive such a communication. Overall, the spirit of this principle has been upheld by the courts. It appears that the courts will not usually intervene in respect of domestic decisions and cannot demand explanations. If reasons are given, however, the courts reserve the right to consider their sufficiency. It may be said that normally decisions of a committee made in accordance with the rules, and made fairly, cannot be overturned.

In conclusion, therefore, what is said in committee should not be repeated outside the confines of a committee meeting, and committee Minutes should remain confidential.

## General

## Political Meetings

Meetings, public or private, can be held in a permanent political club in support of parliamentary and local candidates and a room can be used as a committee room during parliamentary and local elections. For this purpose, a permanent political club can be taken as one which requires as its qualification for membership the furtherance of certain political views.

## Sub-Clubs

No sub-clubs should be formed, or exist, without the permission of the General Committee. In view of possible liability falling on the parent club in connection with such subsidiaries, a member of the General Committee should fill some executive position on the sub-club and report on its affairs, when so desired, at meetings of the 'supreme authority.' All officers of sub-clubs who handle money should be insured by them for fidelity. (see 'Fidelity Insurance.') Clubs should avoid attempting to run credit unions, substantial savings clubs.

# PART TWO – 'HOW TO' GUIDES

## A Series of Practical Guides for Those Operating Members' Clubs

### 1.0 How to Control Cash and Stop Staff Theft

### CASH CONTROL

#### Till systems & cash security

The types of till in operation range from a simple electronic till, a pre-set style of electronic till, to an EPOS (Electronic Point of Sale) system, which is a computerised till with keypad input. The EPOS systems usually provide extensive management information, which helps control all aspects of the club, including petty cash expenditure.

It is important to use the right till system for your club. A good till system should:

- Help to prevent or overcome fraudulent practices, pilfering and carelessness by staff

- Give the management committee sufficient information to run the club efficiently

- Give the management committee information appropriate for the size and type of the club.

Basic electronic till

- Records every transaction

- Totals takings by session, day, and week

- Is simple and easy to use

- Keeps cash safe

- Inexpensive to purchase.

Pre-set electronic till

- Identifies products and cash

- Can assist in stock control

- Keeps cash safe

- Allows multiple users.

## EPOS

- Monitors sales by individual members of staff
- Monitors sales by time
- Password protection and server identification and controls
- Keeps cash safe
- Financial reporting including:
    - Records cash tendered
    - Monitors product groups and controls stock
    - Aid order production from stock and usage
    - Can be linked to a centralised computer
    - Can be accessed from another site
    - Staff payroll and scheduling
    - Staff records
    - Food ordering and kitchen management
    - Records cash expenditure

## Till opening, operation and closing

Till opening, operation and closing procedures will vary in each club depending on the system in place. However, there are general guidelines which staff should follow.

Staff may be responsible for ensuring there is enough cash available in the till for each opening time. The cash in the till at the beginning of a session is known as the 'float'.

- Ensure that staff check that at the beginning of each session there is change in the float, and a small selection of notes
- It is common practice to have an identified amount in the till at the beginning of each day, and to require team members to check that this amount is in the till.

The till drawers may need to be emptied or rotated throughout the opening hours to keep cash secure, and levels of change will need to be checked periodically to avoid any disruption to service.

Till operating procedures should be in writing to make sure everyone is trained to follow the same procedure and is aware of their responsibilities. In a club, where several people may use the till over the course of a session, there will be fewer mistakes and bad practice reduced or avoided.

Operating procedures should cover till handover. If staff handover to each other when changing shifts, they need to explain:

- Any known errors in processing payments or using the tills

- Whether any bills are 'open' in order to prevent non-payment by customers. Having standard operating procedures makes it more difficult for people to be dishonest.

### Cash control and staff theft

There are common fraudulent practices in respect of cash in clubs and other premises that sell alcohol:

### Theft of money

- 'Direct theft' of cash leaving a shortage in the till at the end of the session

- 'Over-charging' which enables the till reading and the cash-in-till to match and which isn't discovered by a stocktake

- 'Under-ringing' which enables the till reading and the cash-in-till to match, but which is discovered later as a result of a stocktake

**'Direct theft'** - taking money out of the till and passing it over the bar to an accomplice.

**'Over-charging'** - a bar person overcharging the customer and keeping the difference between the cash taken from the customer and the value of the sale that has been rung into the till. For example: the bar person rings-in the correct amount, say, £9.50 and asks the customer for £11.50. If the customer queries the amount the bar person pretends it is just a mistake and takes the correct money. Otherwise this is direct theft of £2.00 from the customer rather than the club. The till will be right at the end of the session and so will the stock.

**'Under-ringing'** - a bar person registering less money in the till than is actually taken off the customer. For example, a customer orders and pays for four pints of lager but the bar person only rings-in three pints. The value of the under-ring is placed in the tips jar or passed over the bar to an accomplice.

Use of an efficient cash control system will ensure management is quickly aware of any discrepancies between sales, stock and what is in the till. Ensure that staff ring-in all sales and that they are aware of and follow workplace procedure for recording errors, to ensure accurate till readings.

Even the most sophisticated till systems are only as good as the information that is entered. It is, therefore, essential that every member of the team understands the implications of the way they use the till.

Modern tills can identify the member of staff using the till for each transaction, which can help identify the source of any inaccuracy in the till contents. Alternatively, it may be possible to allocate individuals to separate tills.

## Staff theft counter measures

**Direct theft** – this tends to happen in the first half of a long shift where there is a change of staff halfway through, but no till check – the second group of staff get the blame.

**Counter measure:** put in a fresh till drawer and float at staff changeover and do a till reading and cash check. Any discrepancies can then be attributed to staff going off duty.

**Over-charging & under-ringing** – this can happen at any time. It doesn't show-up at the end of the session, but only as a deficit when the stocktake is done.

**Counter measure:** If you have stock deficits, put in a watcher to observe whether he is being charged correctly. Do regular 'spot checks' and till drawer changes during the course of the session.

If there is a significant surplus of cash compared with the till reading, it probably means the 'under-rings' have not been removed yet. Watch the tips jar.

## General cash-security measures

Do not allow staff:

- To take handbags or coats behind the bar – lock them in the office. If staff need to access to toilets, handbags or sanitary products the steward takes them to the office and can thereby know they're leaving the bar for a legitimate purpose – not to pass money to an accomplice

- To serve members of their own families or friends – another member of staff should do so

- To come into the club on their night off. Try to avoid employing bar staff who are club members or the friends or family of club members

## Handling cash

General guidelines should be given to staff to ensure that they deal securely with cash. Operators need to check that staff collect payment according to the guidelines:

- Staff should tell the customer the price they are expected to pay

- Check the amount that the customer tenders

- When putting the cash into the till, take care to put the right denomination of coin/note into the right section in the till drawer in order to avoid giving more, or less change than is needed

- If change is required, make sure the change is counted back to the customer

- Issue a receipt if required

Occasionally a customer may complain about payment, alleging they have been short-changed or overcharged.

Each club should determine who has the authority to resolve these situations and the procedure for how they should be dealt with. Usually a senior member of staff deals with payment queries. Whatever choice is made, ensure that all team members are aware of the procedure and who can deal with payment queries.

## Staff control

The club steward must ensure that all staff are aware of security, and of the importance of confidential information remaining confidential from anyone outside the business, including their friends and family.

Confidential information can include:

- Financial information about the club or its business performance

- Security information about who does the banking, when and where banking is done, who holds security keys or alarm codes

- Information, such as salaries, staffing or product margins

- Information about other staff, such as their telephone numbers, addresses or work schedules

- Financial details, which may be used in fraud

Staff should be made aware that none of the above information should be discussed with customers – it may be considered a disciplinary offence.

By involving every member of the team in the financial controls and security of the club, and in regular business performance reviews, the management committee and club steward can ensure greater team ownership of payment control.

## 2.0 How to Control Stock

### Introduction

### Why is stocktaking necessary?

The answer to this may seem obvious: to keep track of beverage alcohol products to ensure there is always enough product to satisfy customer demand without having too much that takes up valuable storage space. However, there are some important added bonuses to stock-takes for a club. It reveals how the club's bar is coping financially, where losses are occurring, how much each pour should cost, and which products are popular, and which should not be on the menu. To calculate the usage of inventory, the stock count for the beginning and the end of the period is needed as well as the amount of received inventory stock during the period. Once these variables are known, they are inserted into the following formula:

Opening Stock + Deliveries – Remaining Stock = Stock Sold.

### Ordering stock

Once your usage is known, it is easier to estimate what and how much inventory stock is needed to ensure the bar remains stocked throughout the period. When ordering, estimate usage for the stocktaking period – a week or a month – then calculate whether what is left on ordering day is enough to get you through to delivery day, and then top up stock remaining to the level of stock use plus a little extra to take account of variations of consumption.

### Delivery of stock

Try to do your ordering and accept your deliveries on the same day each week. You might, for example, order on a Monday and accept deliveries on a Thursday. In this way your stocktaking periods are consistent and deliveries predictable.

Count stock in on delivery and always check the delivery against the delivery note. Don't sign a delivery note until you have done so and ensure that any short delivery is noted on the delivery note before you sign it and get the delivery driver to countersign.

Keep all delivery notes for the stocktaker and to cross-check against invoices.

## How should a bar's inventory be counted?

This is the tricky part of the process. Counting a bar's inventory is more complicated than some other industries as it involves counting vessels which may be part full. To ensure the counting is accurate, it should be conducted the same way each time and there should be consistent stock taking periods, only count when the bar is closed and ensure 'counters' are trained properly.

## Spirits and wines

Count spirit and wine bottles and part-bottles in categories – whisky, gin, vodka, wines etc., recording on the stock inventory sheet. Count whole bottles followed by using 'tenthing' for part bottles. This is the process of visually dividing the bottle into tenths and counting how many tenths of liquid remain. Ensure this method of counting is done for the stock cupboard and for each area of the bar so that the total is as accurate as possible. Find the sum of all the totals for the different products and then repeat this process in the exact same manner at the end of the period, allowing a relatively accurate usage total to be obtained.

## Draught beer, lager, and cider

When counting draught beer, lager, and cider, you first count full barrels and estimate the content of part-full barrels that are connected to the beer lines. Many stocktakers are very experienced at doing this but you can do it accurately by weighing. Weigh an empty barrel, then weigh a full one. The difference is the weight of the beer in the barrel. In this way you're able to estimate how many gallons are in a barrel by weighing it and subtracting the weight of the barrel from the total weight. Portable barrel weighing machines can be purchased.

## Counting full bottles of beer and soft drinks

Counting must take place in the cellar and the bar. The process is the same:

Opening Stock + Deliveries – Closing Stock = Stock Sold.

## Choosing the System

Accurate inventory management is achievable with a range of systems, provided as counting is done properly, and the system is used appropriately. This means, if you choose to use pen, paper and purchase orders or even inventory management software, then you can have your inventory in good control. The key is to be consistent and accurate in counting and estimating and to have well-trained and trustworthy staff so that incompetence, breakage or theft can easily be picked up, isolated and dealt with.

## Inventory Management Systems

Many bars do in fact still use pen and paper records for inventory management with remarkable success, however inventory management software can certainly make the job a lot more straightforward.

Controlling your stock is essential in order to:

- Achieve your margins
- Prevent staff or delivery theft
- Rotate stock on a fist-in/first-out basis (FIFO)
- Ensure that cashflow is not tied-up in stock

Crucial to these tasks is the role of the stocktaker.

## The role of the stocktaker

- Will do stock count
- Will produce a written report (computer)
- Inform of stock losses / surplus
- Value of stock at any one time
- Assists in keeping stock to a minimum and reducing impact of purchasing on cashflow
- Will inform GP% and advise on pricing
- Reduces the risk of theft going unnoticed

Stock control is essential to the success of your club as a business.

The stocktaker's main tasks are:

- To ensure that you are making the correct GP margins on every item sold, and in respect of your total wet and/or dry sales

- To advise whether your stocks are 'up' or 'down', i.e., whether your actual cash takings exceed the stocktaker's estimate – 'up' – or whether the estimate of what you should have taken is exceeds your actual takings – 'down' – before taking account of ullage

- If you are using a free-flow delivery system for draught beer in combination with brim-measure glasses, then your actual takings should exceed your stocktaker's estimate by between 2% and 5% after ullage has been subtracted

- If your actual takings exceed your stocktaker's estimate this is known as the 'overage'

### How does the 'overage' arise?

A pint of beer is 20 fluid ounces. When poured into a brim-measure glass that can contain exactly 20 fluid ounces the actual amount of liquid will be less than this amount to allow for the 'head' on the beer. Customers expect a head, but best practice is that when the head has collapsed the remaining liquid should be no less than 95% of the pint measure, in other words 19 fluid ounces. The remaining 5%, or one fluid ounce, accrues in the barrel as an overage that traditionally is used to defray the cost of wastage or 'ullage'.

### What are the implications of a stock deficit?

It depends how large it is. A small stock deficit can simply be a consequence of lax practices in respect of controlling waste or over-pouring. A significant stock deficit is usually the result of theft.

Theft of stock can take place in several different ways.

### Theft of stock:

- At delivery

- From the stock cupboard

- From behind the bar

## Formula for taking stock

| | £ |
|---|---|
| Opening stock | 5,000 |
| + Goods in | 7,000 |
| - Closing Stock | 4,000 |
| = Cost of sales | 8,000 |
| Sales | 16,000 |
| - Cost of sales | 8,000 |
| = Gross profit | 8,000 |

$$\frac{GP}{SALES} \times \frac{100}{1} = GP\%, \text{ e.g., } \frac{8,000}{16,000} \times \frac{100}{1} = 50\%$$

Good stock management has several benefits:

- Ensuring products are available when and where they are wanted, helping to keep customers satisfied

- Keeping stock loss to a minimum to save money, reducing the risk of theft going unnoticed

- Setting standards for stock control will encourage staff to take care with the quality of drinks they sell and to avoid waste

- Employment of a trained stocktaker can ensure the operator knows exactly how much money is tied up in stock – and keep that to a minimum to release cashflow

In your club controlling the security of stock is essential to avoid loss of profit through inefficiency or theft.

The key areas to monitor and control are:

- Deliveries
- When in storage
- When on sale

## Storage

Once deliveries have been accepted it is important to ensure they are immediately taken to their relevant place of storage – particularly so for expensive and/or perishable goods.

Good practise for security and maintaining condition of stock should include:

- Lock storerooms or cupboards and back of premises exits
- Keep keys out of locks and determine which staff members will have responsibility for them
- Regular stock counts of key lines
- Keep doors, which lead into private or staff areas closed
- Train staff to be alert and challenge suspicious customer behaviour
- Train staff to ask for appropriate identification from anyone who wants access to secure areas
- Regular checking of refrigeration temperature where necessary
- Applying appropriate stock rotating principles – FIFO.

**Goods on sale**

At some stage goods will be transferred from storage to the point of sale. Some establishments have a procedure that records goods in and out of storage areas. Only responsible and trained staff should have access to this system. Having a tracking system creates an audit trail for you or your stocktaker to check.

The following are accepted good practises when maintaining security and control in the customer service area:

- Staff should be trained to ensure correct stock rotation, appropriate quantities/measures/weights/items and standards are dispensed
- Records should be kept and/or reported relating to wastage, damaged or soiled goods
- Back up stock is secure
- Service area is not left unattended
- Staff are trained and follow the business policies regarding personal possessions in the customer service area and 'sampling'.

**3.0 How to Understand Your Club's Finances**

**Financial controls**

Getting 'the numbers' right is the key to running a successful club. Understanding basic business percentages will enable you to know whether you are spending too much on wages and fixed costs or whether your gross profit margin is enough to cover your costs and give you a profit/surplus.

Financial controls are crucial. The purpose of financial controls is to enable you to:

- Manage cashflow
- Control costs
- Design a pricing structure
- Plan to make a profit

The key instruments of financial control involve accurate bookkeeping and stocktaking and an understanding of key concepts:

- Profit and loss
- Breakeven point
- Gross profit and net profit
- Product costing and pricing

## Accountancy services

The extent to which an accountant or a bookkeeper will provide you with services will depend upon your own skills and preferences.

An accountant will assist you with:

- Choosing a bookkeeping system
- Preparing VAT returns
- Operating your payroll (wages, tax, and NI)
- Profit and loss accounting monthly/quarterly/annually
- Business and cashflow forecasting
- Advice on pricing
- Preparation and submission of annual tax returns

## Who requires access to your bookkeeping or accounts?

- Your accountant
- Your stocktaker
- HMRC

- Your bank
- Department of Employment
- Courts of Law/Employment Tribunals

**What do you need to record?**

**Income** – bar, food, room hire, machines

**Expenditure** – cash and cheque payments, e.g., wages, suppliers

**Banking** – cash, cheque, credit/debit cards, BACS

## Terminology

To understand and to control your club's finances you need to understand some basic terminology and how to make some simple calculations.

---

*Definitions:*

**Retail price:** what the customer pays including VAT.

**Sales price:** the cost of the product excluding VAT.

**Cost of sales or cost price:** the cost of the product excluding VAT.

**Gross profit:** the sales price – the cost price.

**Net profit:** gross profit – other business expenses.

**VAT:** 'value added tax' collected on behalf of HMRC.

**Fixed costs:** business costs that always remain the same, e.g., rent.

**Variable costs:** costs that vary with the volume of the business, e.g., wages

---

## Profit & Loss Account (P&L Account)

A profit and loss account is a snapshot of a business' performance.

- Used in conjunction with cashflow forecasts and break-even analysis it is useful for determining the courses of action required to maintain or attain profitability

- It can highlight where costs are too high and how the business is performing against its P&L forecast

- Usually determined as an annual account, it can be done over shorter periods of time and it details what sales have been achieved, at what GP, less overheads to give an overall NP figure (before tax)

Aim to base your income and cost percentages on the following model:

|  | %age |
|---|---|
| Sales Income: | 100 |
| Less: Cost of Sales: | 50 |
| Less rent/mortgage: | 10 |
| Less wages: | 10 |
| Less other costs: | 20 |
| = Net Profit: | 10 |

As in the example below:

**Try this exercise:**

Sales (net of VAT) 12,000 (100%)

| - Cost price | 6,000 (50%) |
|---|---|
| = Gross profit | |
| - Rent | 1,200 (10%) |
| - Wages: | 1,200 (10%) |
| - Other costs: | 2,400 (20%) |
| = Net profit | |

### Differences between P&L and cashflow

Cash flow is the movement of money in and out of the club. It is useful when planning the funding requirements of the club, either on a short or long-term basis, by forecasting the cash that is expected to come in and go out of the account.

On the other hand, profit & loss is the effect of all the cash movement i.e., the levels of sales less thelevels of overheads will equate to the overall profit/ surplus of the club.

## Profit & Loss Account

This example of a Profit and Loss Account shows how it can be applied to the sales and expenses of a club over a 12 months' period:

| P&L ACCOUNT | |
| --- | --- |
| **Takings** | 250,000 (Gross Sales) |
| Less VAT | 41,666 (VAT Output) |
| = | 208,334 (Net Sales) |
| *less* **Cost of Sales** | 104,167 |
| = | 104,167 (Gross Profit) |
| *less* **Overheads/Expenses:** | |
| rent | 20,833 |
| wages | 16,667 |
| rates | 2,000 |
| insurance | 3,000 |
| electricity/gas | 8,000 |
| telephone/broadband | 1,000 |
| cleaning materials | 3,000 |
| bank charges | 2,000 |
| professional fees | 5,000 |
| motor exp | 2,500 |
| repairs & renewals/equipment | 10,000 |
| print/post | 2,000 |
| advertising | 5,000 |
| sundries | 3,167 |
| **Total Overheads** | 84,167 |

£104,167 (GP) - £84,167 (overheads) = £20,000 (Net Profit before tax)

**Cash flow** - A cash flow statement is similar to the profit and loss account. The difference between the two is that the cash flow statement shows the figures including VAT and shows the sales and expenses 'flow' in and out of the club over time. This allows you to predict when the club may be short of funds and may require an overdraft facility. Or the statement may show when funds are likely to be available for new purchases. It can be easily produced on a computer and updated on a weekly basis. It may be that an accountant could assist in producing cash flow statements and keeping them up to date.

Break-even point - The break-even point is vital in understanding whether a club should put on a 'special' or a 'regular' event, as well as in helping you to understand how profitable the club is on a daily basis.

The break-even point is the point at which all running costs have been covered without making either a profit or loss. It is a way of calculating the volume of sales required just to keep the club running. Any amount above this level gives a profit and below puts the business in a loss situation.

## A cashflow forecast

| Income In £ | Open | Jan | Feb | March | April | May | June |
|---|---|---|---|---|---|---|---|
| Sales | | 3,000 | 3,000 | 3,800 | 4,000 | 4,000 | 4,200 |
| Capital In | 10,000 | | | | | | |
| Total Income | 10,000 | 3,000 | 3,000 | 3,800 | 4,000 | 4,000 | 4,200 |
| **Finances/Assets** | | | | | | | |
| Loan Repayment | | 100 | 100 | 100 | 100 | 100 | 100 |
| Interest Paid | | 10 | 10 | 10 | 10 | 10 | 10 |
| Total Finances/Assets | 0 | 110 | 110 | 110 | 110 | 110 | 110 |
| **Direct Costs** | | | | | | | |
| Materials | | | 150 | 150 | 150 | 150 | 150 |
| Labour | | | 300 | 300 | 300 | 300 | 300 |
| Total Costs | | 0 | 450 | 450 | 450 | 450 | 450 |
| **Expenses** | | | | | | | |
| Salary | | | 1,000 | 1,000 | 1,000 | 1,000 | 1,000 |
| Office Rent | | | 100 | 100 | 100 | 100 | 100 |
| Telephone | | | | | 100 | 100 | 100 |
| Utilities | | | | 100 | | | 100 |
| Insurance | | | 100 | 100 | 100 | 100 | 100 |
| Total Expenses | 0 | 1,200 | 1,300 | 1,300 | 1,300 | 1,400 | 1,300 |
| **Opening Balance** | 0 | 10,000 | 11,240 | 12,480 | 12,480 | 12,480 | 12,480 |
| Total Income | 10,000 | 3,000 | 3,000 | 3,500 | 3,800 | 4,000 | 4,200 |
| Total Outgoings | 0 | 1,760 | 1,860 | 1,960 | 1,960 | 2,060 | 1,960 |
| Net Cashflow | 10,000 | 1,240 | 1,140 | 1,540 | 1,840 | 1,940 | 2,240 |

In the above cashflow forecasts the ending balance is therefore £2,240.

## Reading the cash-flow

Now that you have produced a forecast cash-flow, what should you be looking for?

**Net cash-flow** - If it is negative or consistently close to nil, the business will struggle to make a profit – you need to take actions to improve your position.

**Closing/End Balance** - If it is on a downward trajectory then you need to take action to arrest the decline – when the closing balance is negative due to large payments in that month, e.g., VAT, this is when you will need bank financing to assist with cash-flow by means of an overdraft facility.

## Actions on the back of cash-flow

**Banking facilities** - If your cash-flow dictates that you will require assistance at certain times, ask the bank to help you by showing them your forecast – most banks will look favourably on your request as you are demonstrating sound financial awareness.

**Smoothing cash-flow** - Set up direct debits where possible in order to avoid large payments going out in one particular month, or using your forecast make one-off payments when the cashflow can sustain it.

**Temporary cash injection** - Put cash into the business in order to help with tight cash-flow periods – you do this on the basis that this cash will be taken back out of the business.

**Permanent cash injection** - Obviously opposite of above, whereby the cash will not be withdrawn from the business, but ensure you are not just propping up a failing business temporarily. Looking at the net cash-flow and closing/end balance which are strong, will demonstrate that your business has a better chance of success.

## Calculating the sales price and retail price from the cost price

You must know:

- The cost price, and
- Target GP%.

Cost + GP = Sales Price (net of VAT).

Assume: cost price of £1.04 and target GP of 50%: £1.04 ÷ .50 = £2.08 (sales price).

£2.08 x 1.20 (to add VAT) = £2.50 (retail price)

Retail price - VAT = sales price.

e.g., £2.50 (RP) ÷ 1.2 (to remove VAT) = £2.08 sales price net of VAT

Sales price - cost price = gross profit.

e.g., £2.08 - £1.04 = £1.04 GP

GP ÷ by sales price x 100 = GP%.

£1.04 ÷ £2.08 x 100 = 50% GP

## VALUE ADDED TAX

### Introduction

All businesses that have a turnover of over £85,000 (accurate for businesses submitting accounts for 2019/2020) are required to register for VAT and maintain appropriate records. Several different schemes are available from HMRC to account for VAT payments, as well as a variety of payment methods.

Appropriate information about making the right choice for a business can be obtained through accountants and/or HMRC.

The main schemes for small businesses are:

**Annual accounting** -The annual accounting scheme allows the business to complete just one VAT return each year, instead of the usual four. It will make instalment payments of the VAT that it expects to owe, so that they are not faced with a large VAT bill at the end of the year.

**Cash accounting** - Under the cash accounting scheme the business accounts for VAT based on payments received and made, rather than on invoices issued and received.

It is important to remember to deduct VAT from the takings when calculating the club's share of the gross profit as failure to account for VAT is one of the most common reasons for the collapse of small businesses.

In order to avoid confusing the VAT income that will be paid to HMRC, and the businesses gross income, the VAT element of sales should be regularly subtracted (usually weekly)and that sum put into a separate bank account, to ensure it does not become part of the cash flow.

Small businesses sometimes keep separate VAT books that list incoming invoices, clearly showing the VAT element, and cash sales figures and other income, with the VAT element clearly indicated. As these figures will be audited, all invoices and cash receipt records must be kept.

## Calculating VAT returns

### Try this exercise:

To calculate a retail price a retailer needs to add a percentage which represents the current VAT rate.

**Adding VAT to sales price:**

SALES PRICE   +   VAT      = RETAIL PRICE
(VAT exclusive)                    (VAT inclusive)

Sales Price x 1.2 = Retail Price, e.g., SP: £1.00 x 1.20 = £1.20

**Subtracting VAT from retail price:**

RETAIL PRICE    ÷  1.2       = SALES PRICE
(VAT inclusive)                    (VAT exclusive)

Retail Price ÷ by 1.20 = Sales Price, e.g., £1.20 ÷ 1.2 = £1.00

**Calculating the VAT element of a VAT-inclusive price:**

Retail Price - Sales Price = VAT, e.g., £1.20 - £1.00 = £0.20 pence

OR

Retail Price ÷ 6 = VAT, e.g., £1.20 ÷ 6 = £0.20 pence

## VAT calculations

| | £ |
|---|---|
| Output Tax<br>(VAT collected from customers) | 7962.50 |
| -    Input Tax<br>(VAT spent on business purchases) | 2904.25 |
| = VAT to be paid or claimed | 5058.25 |

## 4.0    How to Do Merchandising, Presentation & Pricing

## What is merchandising?

> ### *Important definitions*
>
> "Visual merchandising is the activity of promoting the sale of goods, especially by their presentation, in retail outlets." Oxford English dictionary.
>
> "The means by which you improve sales and profitability at the point of sale." Anon.
>
> "The art of silent selling." Anon.

### Growing turnover and profits

There are three ways in which you can grow the turnover and profits of your club; by increasing:

1. Footfall

2. Spend per head, and

3. Dwell-time

**Advertising and marketing** are the means by which you increase footfall.

Merchandising is the means by which you maximise spend per head and dwell-time, in respect of the customer traffic that advertising and marketing generates.

Merchandising involves combining your products, space, and the environment into an appealing and stimulating display which is designed for the purpose of driving more customers in your club towards the bar or other points of sale, and the products you want to sell to them.

Merchandising is carried out to:

- Promote impulse buying

- Promote new products

- Move old stock

- Increase the sale of particular products

- Encourage new customers

- Increase the frequency of visits

## Developing a merchandising strategy

The best way to develop a merchandising strategy is to consider the customer journey; literally, the journey from arrival just outside the club, to entry and then the progress of the customer through the club to the bar or other 'point of sale'. Think also of all the other movements the customer might make whilst in the club – to a table, the carvery or other food display, the toilets etc. – and plan your communication with the customer with all these movements in mind.

## Areas of opportunity - exterior and entrance

Ensuring that the exterior and entrance of the club is clean and tidy and that the signage, banners and A-boards reflect the offering inside the club is very important. The exterior is the first impression that the customer has of the club. The old adage "you never get a second chance to make a first impression" is no less true for being old! The best way to think of this is as a 'decision-making corridor':

## The Decision-making corridor

- Communicate with the customer from the beginning
- Externally: Windows, A-boards and Menu Box
- Route to the bar: lobby, pillars and ceiling
- Bar: torso level, near tills and on the bar staff
- After purchase: route to toilets, near DJ, near TV
- Tables
- Toilets
- Near door exit

## Some Key Facts

Research into buying decisions in alcohol-licensed premises indicates:

- You have 3 seconds to obtain people's attention.
- 60% of buying decisions are made at the point of purchase.
- 35% of consumers are influenced in choice of drink by product merchandising.
- The average attention span at the point of purchase is 11 seconds.
- 34% of female consumers never visit the bar.

## The route to the bar

It takes approximately 14 seconds to walk from the entrance to the bar in most club premises. What kind of messages will you communicate to customers along the route, and where will you place them?

Location of signs and posters:

- Lobby
- Pillars
- Ceiling

Messages:

- Short – 5 to 10 words
- Where to go and how to order, e.g., how to place a food order, where the toilets are

## Signs and posters and the psychology of communication

To merchandise effectively, you need to understand how gender and personality differences affect how people communicate, and how receptive they are to merchandising and messaging.

**Gender differences** – research suggests men and women generally think and communicate differently.

**Men:** generally don't like to ask for directions. This is because they are often status conscious and tend to think and speak 'vertically':

"Did what I say make you think higher or lower of me?"

To ask for directions is to admit you do not know. Most men are not comfortable with this because it may make someone think less of them. Therefore, when they enter a club, they need to see the bar, or if they are coming to dine, or need to visit the toilet first, they look for a sign or poster that tells them where to go and what to do.

So, signs and posters are an important way of communicating with men:

- Tell them what they need to do to place a food order or direct them to the bar
- Direct them to the toilet, so that they don't have to ask
- And then in any of the corridors of travel that you are directing them along, place merchandising messages along the route

**Women:** tend to think and speak 'horizontally':

"Does what I say draw me in closer or push me away?"

To ask for help is to get drawn into the inner circle. If a woman in a club doesn't know where to go she looks for a person, not a sign.

But not all women…

**Personality differences** – 'extrovert' and 'introvert'.

Introverts are also sign readers. Introverts are people who want information before interaction. They want knowledge before they speak to someone. And then they need time to process that knowledge. Signs are their best friends because signs answer their basic questions before they have to interact with someone. Signs also help them formulate new questions they may need to ask. Therefore, 75% of the population (all men and half the women) are served by signs and posters. A good sign or poster is one that answers questions. It gives the right amount of information in a quick and easy-to-read format. Sometimes the only question is "how much?" More often the question is "why?"

### Point of sale – bar and back of bar

The point of sale is the time and place at which a customer commits to a purchase. Your points of sale need to be arranged literally from the point of view of the customer. Approximately 60% of purchases made in retail shops are accounted for by impulse buying. Whilst many customers will enter the club knowing what they are going to order, many will only make their buying decision at the bar.

### Back of bar displays

The main rules are:

- Keep the back bar free of clutter
- Concentrate on displaying high margin product in key areas
- Ensure that there is a simple selling message or call to action
- Remember that you are trying to prompt purchase

### Eye-level is Buy-level

Vertically people look from eye-level to just below the chin. Horizontally people's normal field of vision is about 6 feet, and they look from left to right (that's how we were all taught to read).

## What "draws the eye"?

When presented with a display the gaze of the customer is first drawn to the centre of the display, and then the display is 'read' from left to right. Breaking up displays into "easy-to-read" sequences is an important way of merchandising products. It reflects the psychology of human perception and how we process sequences.

For example, most people, if they read a sequence of numbers can retain and recite about 6 digits without having to read it again. Which of the two following ways of writing down a mobile phone number would be easiest to read and remember?

# 07971284031 Or 0797 128 4031

## Bottles on optic

Likewise, with bottles on optic, if your display of optics is too long, customers will become confused; they will not take it in. The normal field of vision is about 6 feet, and so customers will focus on the centre, optic number five.

The majority of customers look from left to right. In a display of four optics the left one (1) will be strong, but the right one (4) will be the strongest, because that is the end of the "sentence" – where the eye comes to rest.

So, when deciding how to display your bottles on optic, break up the "sentence" of display into smaller "phrases". Display two groups of four bottles rather than a continuous display of eight bottles:

With two groups the bottles to the left and right of each group will be strong (1 & 4 and 5 & 8). In this way you can maximise the number of premium brands that you want the customer to notice and select, or the new products you are promoting, or the high GP products – whatever your sales priority is.

Fridge merchandising

- The key to merchandising fridge space is to keep it simple
- Make it easy for customers to see the products that you want them to buy
- Use horizontal block facings to promote high GP items at the top of the fridge

- Skips with ice can be used to keep high volume items cold on busy nights
- Fruit juices can be kept on ambient shelves as they are usually served with ice
- Use the plan below as a guide to maximising GP

## Top shelf - excitement generators

These are new branded products that excite interest – the customer can see that the product range does change. Or, they may be seasonal products that the customer may buy on impulse, e.g., pear cider for summer appeal.

## Middle shelf – cash generators

Well established big volume brands that contribute a significant share of sales and profit. These are *'must-stock' brands that the customer will simply expect to find behind the bar* – Budweiser, Becks.

## Bottom shelf – turf protectors

These are relatively low volume brands that meet specific customer needs and need to be stocked to maintain customer loyalty, e.g., Holsten Pils, Stella low alcohol- or alcohol-free lagers.

## Hot spots and product promotion

Merchandising 'hot spots' are places where customers naturally look. The back of the bar is an example. Hot spots should be reserved for products you really want to promote.

They include the:

- Arrival point
- Back bar fitting
- Optic rail
- Space above the till
- Right-hand-side of the field of vision, particularly to the right of the till
- Top bottle shelf
- Front bar counter

## Back bar fitting

- This is a natural hot spot. Use it for:
- posters
- stickers
- product placement when engaged in a promotion

## The merchandising matrix

- The customer only registers certain information at certain times
- Research shows that messages should be seven words or less
- Complex information should be communicated to the customer when they are at the table or in
- the toilets

## The matrix explained

### 'A' Boards

Exterior chalkboards – attract passing trade, educate passing trade for future.

### Should advertise:

- Most appealing offers to attract new customers (2-4-1 promotion, Meal Deals)
- High cash generating aspects of the business (function room/hotel rooms)

## Lightboxes

Exterior wall mounted boxes which are lit.

### Should advertise:

- Menus (expected to be seen here, menus not shown may lead customers to the conclusion that food isn't available)
- Photographs (if applicable, of function rooms, hotel rooms)

## Window posters

Double sided posters in clear vinyl wallets suspended from hooks by suction pads. A maximum of 25% of window space should be utilised for posters.

**Should advertise:**

- Value offer where applicable
- Aspects of the business which are a point of difference to competitors on the high street

**Postcard racks**

These are stylish postcard racks which hold a maximum of 6 types of postcards/flyers. They should be situated on the toilet route. All offers can be advertised here for customer perusal at a place where traffic passes frequently.

**Should advertise (where applicable):**

- Duplicates of A6 flyers
- Mini cocktail menus
- Takeaway food menus
- Sports listings
- Info on hotel & function rooms

**Poster frames (lobby)**

Hot spot which all customers are likely to pass, therefore ensuring maximum exposure for contents.

**Should advertise:**

- Specifics for sports fixtures
- Specifics of entertainment, e.g., band listings, part/event nights

**Poster frames (bar walls)**

Secondary point of focus for customers (not part of the dissection walk).

**Should advertise (where applicable):**

- Accommodation and function room posters
- Sports and entertainments listings

**Poster frames (route to toilets)**

This route is frequented by the majority of customers and is usually a well-lit area.

Should advertise (where applicable):

- Sports fixtures and entertainments listings
- Quiz Night details, function room and accommodation details

## Poster frames (in toilets)

Captured market.

**Should advertise:**

- Value drink offer
- Sports fixtures
- Specifics of entertainment, e.g., band listings, party/event nights.

## Telephone (poster frame nearby)

Captured market.

**Should advertise:**

- Sports listings.

Posters always in frames.

## Bar top

This is the point of service and therefore receives maximum exposure. It can be useful for impulse purchasing and upselling.

Should advertise (where applicable):

- Food menus
- Cocktail menus
- Food offers
- Upselling offers

## Till fronts

Another point of service, although variable fronts in all outlets. Also restricted with POS designs.

**Should advertise:**

- Cash-back facility and high GP product awareness teasers

## Tables

Customers have time to digest information placed before them on the tables. Flyers can be informative and detailed. Either Perspex stands or wooden blocks can be used to house A6 flyers.

Take care, however, not to crowd the table with too much information, it can and will look messy and not be as informative.

**Should advertise:**

- Food menus, cocktail menus (where applicable)
- No smoking cards, sport and entertainment listings
- Other cards from the marketing dept which are applicable to the outlet

## Chalkboards

Chalkboards are used to exploit many messages. They can be traditionally or contemporarily illustrated.

**Remember:**

- Keep them clean, keep all messages up to date, get them illustrated professionally, keep them simple

## Chalkboards (behind the bar)

Perused by the majority of customers in a well-lit area

**Should advertise (where applicable):**

- Cocktail list
- Wine list
- Value drink offers

## Chalkboards (other)

**Should advertise:**

- Food offers
- Sport
- Various entertainments, e.g., Quiz Nights, Comedy Nights,

## PRESENTATION & PRICING

### Product presentation

Products need to be merchandised and presented in an attractive and visible way behind the bar and on the bar counter, and you can influence buying decisions by the words you use to encourage the buying of premium products:

Make sure your merchandising:

- Lets customers know what is available
- When it is available
- What the offer is
- Gives them compelling reasons to want to try the products


### Power, Sizzle and Action Words

- Power words grab people's attention e.g. WIN, FREE, SAVE…
- Sizzle words are descriptive words that stimulate desire e.g. SMOOTH, FRESH…
- Action words are those which motivate purchase e.g. BUY NOW!


### Organising stock

- Beer pumps arranged for easy access
- Bottled products refrigerated
- Bottles wiped and arranged in lines, labels facing outward
- Show the full range of products and move bottles from the back of the fridge so it always looks full
- Fill the fridge from the back to ensure that you always sell the product cooled
- Bold, eye-catching merchandising – point of sale, product displays, chalk boards
- Keep a 'drivers' shelf' of low alcohol and alcohol-free products
- Give prominence to high value, high volume products, e.g., premium beers and ciders
- Dispense products into the correct, branded glasses
- Give attention to glass and optic hygiene

## Pricing strategies

In you club you can set your own prices, although guidance and knowledge of local competition will both be important influences.

## How do you set your drinks' prices?

## Cost-price-plus or category pricing

This is a method of setting prices that takes the cost of buying-in the product and then adds a margin. Often stocktakers will advise on a GP percentage that you need to achieve on each product, given your sales mix, in order to achieve an overall GP percentage of, say, 50%. This tends to lead to category pricing, for example, all fruit juices or mixers being priced the same, or all session beers being priced the same. This simplifies the price proposition but ignores the benefits of 'premiumisation' and the perceived value that customers attach to well-known brands

## Ladder pricing

This is a pricing strategy that recognises that customers are prepared to pay more for premium products. For example: premium strength lagers can attract a higher price than a standard strength lager. Customers expect to pay more.

## Top tip:

You can't bank percentages - a lower GP on a high-priced item may deliver more money in the till than a higher GP on a lower priced item:

$100\% \times 0 = 0$

$0\% \times 1000 = 0$

## Example:

Which is better?

Selling an £8 bottle of wine with a 70% GP, OR

a £15 bottle of wine with a 50% GP?

## Combined or bundle pricing

Research has shown that people spend 14% less on drinks than they intend to spend when they come out. Consider offering a selection of combined price items, for example, any standard spirit and mixer for a combined price. People are looking for value.

# 5.0 How to Deliver Good Customer Service and Efficient Bar Dispense

## Introduction

Good customer service and efficient bar service is key to meeting and exceeding your customers' expectations and to keep them coming back. Although what follows in this guide is about the process of good customer service and efficient bar dispense it is important to understand that customer service is about establishing a culture. Key to this is recognizing that customers do not just attend your club for the drink, food or entertainment, they attend for the whole experience of enjoying a night out.

## The customer service process

### The welcome

When a customer walks into your premises you have only a short time to make the right impression.

Research shows that customers formulate their initial impressions within eight seconds of arrival.

Your welcome should be:

- Warm

- Friendly

- Instructional

All customers arriving at a bar or counter should receive an immediate acknowledgement from staff, even if it is only a smile and nod of greeting! Within 30 seconds you should have verbally acknowledged the customer – "be with you in a just a moment sir". The minimum form of acknowledgement should be eye contact, but ideally acknowledgement should also be verbal.

Staff should:

- Serve customers in order of arriving

- Be friendly, courteous, and helpful always

- Inform the customer of any ordering process or waiting times

- Be alert and watchful for the next customer

- Make use of eye contact and smile

- Speak to customers when directly serving them, e.g., "Sorry to keep you waiting", "Good
- morning, how are you today?"
- Help customers make appropriate choices (know your product range)
- Recognise regular customers and acknowledge them by name
- Provide assistance to elderly or disabled customers

### Taking an order

A customer may require help or advice making choices. Quickly establish the customer's requirements by listening carefully and repeat what the customer has said back to them for the avoidance of doubt. Standard procedures for taking an order will include:

- Listening carefully to avoid mistakes
- Qualify the sale e.g., "Would you like ice and a slice of lemon?"
- Staff having knowledge of the product range
- Establish price range, e.g., "Our red wines range in price from £8 a bottle to £16 a bottle, what did you want to spend?"
- Offer an alternative product if you have not got the precise product the customer wants
- 'Sell up' and offer choices wherever possible, e.g., "So, you want to order the gammon steak, do you want pineapple with that, or a fried egg?"
- Know what products are on 'special offer' and highlight offers
- Establish the method of payment

### Serving products and establishing standards

A standards-led approach to customer service, that puts the customer first, can be illustrated by considering how we can standardise the service process – thereby embedding high standards

### Personal standards

### Personal presentation and hygiene

All staff must be clean and smartly dressed in a manner that conforms to the management's dress code or uniform. Appearance is part of the total product that you are selling the customer.

Remember the maxim: 'People Buy People'.

- Clothes/uniform – clean, ironed and in good repair
- Hair – must be kept clean and tidy. Hair longer than shoulder length should be tied back
- Perfume/aftershave – heavy or strong fragrances should be avoided
- Shoes – clean and polished and only appropriate shoes should be worn
- Hands – must be washed regularly - after visits to the toilet, blowing your nose or smoking.
- Nails should ideally be kept short
- Jewellery – kept to a minimum
- Religious symbols: a sensitive approach needs to be adopted and the display of discreet religious symbols should be allowed

## Premises standards

### The customer area

Remember, customers form an initial impression of your premises within eight seconds of arrival. This known as 'kerb appeal'. All areas to which customers have access should be kept to a high standard:

- Outside areas/car parks kept clean and tidy
- Paintwork must be kept clean and dust free – any chipped paintwork reported to the management
- Walls and wallpaper/paint in good repair – any torn wallpaper or chipped paint reported to the management
- Flooring must be safe, clean, and free from debris or obstructions
- Furniture must be clean, presentable and in good repair
- Curtain arrangements must be clean, dust-free, hanging correctly and safe
- Lamps and light fittings must all be working correctly, light bulbs replaced as necessary and light shades fitted properly
- Ventilation must be working correctly, and all ducts and louvers must be clean and dust-free

- Report immediately any rips or tears in carpets or seating
- All relevant notices must be displayed
- All machines or equipment for the use of children must be safe and in good working order
- The customer area must be kept clean throughout the hours of opening

**The toilets**

- All premises must offer toilet facilities – this is a legal requirement in pubs, bars, and restaurants and increasingly toilet or 'rest room' facilities are made available in other types of retail outlet too
- Toilets should be checked before opening, and throughout the session, to ensure that they are clean, tidy, and stocked with all necessary toiletries
- Toilets should be provided for male, female and disabled customers
- Locks must be working, and broken locks replaced as soon as possible
- Sufficient toilet tissue
- Hand dryers working
- Liquid soap dispensers working and stocked
- Sinks clean and plugs attached with no drip marks around vanity units
- Toilets and urinals clean and checked regularly throughout opening hours
- Paintwork and tiles in good condition and any graffiti removed as soon as possible
- Mirrors and windows clean and unblemished with broken mirrors replaced as soon as possible
- Sanitary bins clean and in good condition
- Dispense machines clean and well stocked
- Rubbish bins clean and regularly emptied
- Fragrance dispensers working and stocked
- All lights working

## The bar or counter

The bar or service counter must be professionally presented at all times:

- Bar or counter must be clean, polished, and clutter-free – and should be regularly cleaned with debris being removed throughout the session

- Point of sale material and any dispense equipment must be sparkling with all brand names facing the customer

- The back bar or counter fitting must be clean with all product displays having impact – the back fitting can be an effective way of merchandising products

- Popular lines should have at least two facings

- Products on shelves should be clean with labels facing the front where customers can see them

- All stock lines must be available and preferably on display - using the vertical method of display wherever possible

- The overall impression of the back bar or counter fitting must be professional, attractive and a good selling point

- All working areas must be clean and safe

- All statutory notices and price lists on display

- Till price display should be visible to the customer

## The farewell

Where possible say goodbye/goodnight to customers as they leave.

- Thank them for their business

- Say you hope to see them again soon

- Enquire where they are going on to home – somewhere else

- Offer directions if appropriate

- Offer to call a taxi if appropriate

## Building safety and fire safety

A safe environment meets an important human need, as well as complying with statutory Requirements. All risk assessments for building and fire safety must be complete and up-to-date.

- All fire exits illuminated and means of escape free from obstruction

- All fire exit doors, crash bars etc., operating properly

- Fire alarm and emergency lighting tests carried out and recorded on a daily basis

- All carpets, curtains, upholstery and fixtures and fittings to comply with fire retardance Regulations

- Employers and public liability insurance in place

- At least one person trained in first aid in the workplace should be in attendance during working hours and a fully stocked first aid box must be available

- All working and public areas must be effectively lit

- Fire drills should be carried out and recorded in line with statutory requirements

## The welcome

| THE STANDARD | THE PROCEDURE | BEST PRACTICE |
|---|---|---|
| The welcome should be warm, friendly, and instructional. | Staff should acknowledge customers within 30 seconds – minimum of eye-contact. | Recognise regular customers and address them be name. |
| It should include telephone enquiries. | Serve customers in order of arrival. | Identify those customers unfamiliar with the premises and offer help. |
| Introduce the customer to the food ordering system, where appropriate | Staff should:<br>• be friendly, courteous, and helpful<br>• be alert and watchful for the next customer<br>• use eye-contact and smile<br>• speak to customers when serving them<br>• inform customers of special offers<br><br>Answering the phone:<br>• give the club name<br>• your name, and<br>• How can I help you? | Suggest elderly or disabled customers sit down, take the order, and serve drinks at the table.<br><br>Indicate where the outside smoking area is. |

## Taking the order

| THE STANDARD | THE PROCEDURE | BEST PRACTICE |
|---|---|---|
| When taking an order you should do so in an efficient manner. | Establish the customer's requirements – listen carefully to avoid mistakes. | Mentally group the order by products, e.g., soft drinks, spirits and mixers, beer – and collect all these at the same time. |
| Staff should have sufficient product knowledge to assist customers with ordering. | Offer ice and a slice. | |
| | Where possible serve draught products last to retain heads. | Always offer ice and a slice. |
| Staff should be aware of upselling opportunities. | Know high margin products and know promotional products - highlight offers. | Use opportunity to sell preferred lines. |
| Drinks must always be served in a hygienic, attractive, and appealing way. | Demonstrate good product knowledge – wine and beer tastes/countries of origin/ABVs. | Sell up where possible. |
| | Serve in correct glass and size for the drink. Use branded glasses where appropriate. | Regular staff training and information sheets. |
| | Use a clean, cold, undamaged glass. Use a fresh glass every serve. Where a customer has his own tankard, dispense into a clean glass, and pour into his vessel away from the dispense area. | Any member of bar staff should be capable of taking an order.

Check glass prior to use. |
| | Do not dip the beer tap into the glass except when the Swan Neck system is in use. | Look for lipstick marks and clean off prior to placing in the glasswasher. |
| | Never use a glass as an ice-scoop – use ice tongs. Locate ice buckets on the back bar. | |
| | Dispense optic by hand to avoid cross-contamination | |
| | Correct spirit measures to be used and washed after every use. | |

| THE STANDARD | THE PROCEDURE | BEST PRACTICE |
|---|---|---|
| Correcting errors | Use government stamped glasses only for draught products dispensed from a free-flow system No more than 5% head on beer. Staff to replace incorrect drinks, e.g., wrong drink served, cloudy beer and advise management. All staff should be aware of complaints procedure. | Pour stouts early and allow to settle. in the glasswasher. |

## The farewell

| THE STANDARD | THE PROCEDURE | BEST PRACTICE |
|---|---|---|
| The end of the evening/visit Thanking the customer: thank the customer in a warm and friendly manner. | The last impression should leave a positive, lasting impression. Face the customer, make friendly eye-contact and thank them for their business. Check the customer has had an enjoyable visit. Continue to work whilst saying goodbye. Whenever you see someone getting ready to leave the table or the pub, always say goodbye. | Advise the customer of any forthcoming events or promotions. |

## 6.0    How To Manage the Cellar

## INTRODUCTION TO THE CELLAR

## WHAT IS BEER?

### How is beer made?

All beers are made in the same way, with the same ingredients. However, it is only at the final production stage that beer is treated in different ways.

The four ingredients which go into all beer are:

1. Water,
2. Hops,
3. Yeast, and
4. Malted barley.

If we are producing cask ale, the beer is run directly into the cask. The beer is unfiltered and unpasteurised. The beer needs to be 'conditioned' (this is explained later) when it is delivered to the pub cellar. As the product is unpasteurised and exposed to air once on sale, it has a limited shelf life, which is three days.

If we are producing beer for a bottle or a keg the beer is 'conditioned' in the brewery and then filtered to remove any sediment. This is called 'bright' beer. The beer is then pasteurised to keep the beer fresher for longer. However, it should be sold within five days of being placed on sale.

Beer is a product that your customers consume. Therefore, it is classified as a food under The Food Safety Act 1990. All beer should be stored in a temperature- controlled cellar.

Be aware of some of the hazards in the cellar. Floors can be slippery when they have been cleaned so make sure a yellow 'Wet Floor' sign is in place to warn others of the dangers.

It is important the cellar is well lit, so ensure strip lights are maintained (covered) and working.

There are extremely strict regulations and procedures in place in our kitchens regarding serving food, and the same rules should apply in the cellar.

These include:

- Hygiene
- Temperature
- Stock Control
- Accepting deliveries

**Hygiene**

The Food Safety Act 1990 states that if you are seen to be putting your customers at risk from infection you can be prosecuted.

A dirty cellar encourages the growth of wild yeast and bacteria that can affect beer quality and ultimately sales. So, the beer cellar should be cleaned thoroughly at least once a week – preferably when stock levels are at their lowest and any beer spillages should be cleaned immediately. In addition, all equipment in the cellar needs to be scrupulously clean, including beer lines, couplers, dipsticks, taps, and floats.

No other food products should be stored in the cellar as it is against food hygiene regulations

## Temperature

One of the key elements which affect beer is the temperature it is stored at. The ideal cellar temperature is between **11°c and 13°c**. This should be checked at least daily by looking at the thermometer.

The cellar temperature is achieved by using fans. These are driven by external donkey engines and are situated on the wall of the cellar and blast out cold air. To make sure these are working efficiently:

- Ensure the grills over the fans are free from dust and debris
- Check around the back of the fans and make sure no ice is present (if so call out engineer)
- Make sure the fans are kept switched on – they have automatic cut-outs to switch them off when cellar temperature is reached
- Ensure the door to the cellar is not left propped open

Beer is directly cooled by remote coolers and you must make sure the coolers are unobstructed.

If the cellar temperature falls below 11°c or rises to above 13°c it can have a serious impact on the way the beer dispenses, causing wastage and dissatisfied customers.

If the cellar is too cold, some beers will dispense flat, cask beers will take longer to condition, and they may go hazy or cloudy.

If the cellar is too warm, some beers may froth when they are dispensed, and cask beers will go off very quickly.

When beer is delivered into the cellar, it takes 24 to 48 hours to reach cellar temperature, depending on weather conditions outside.

To ensure the cellar maintains this temperature, it is essential that the coolers and fans are left on continuously, and they are maintained properly. Once a week, brush the dust and fluff from the grills, and check no ice is forming behind the coolers.

## Stock control and deliveries

Once a delivery note has been signed the beer legally becomes the pubs responsibility – and if there are any discrepancies it becomes difficult to prove. So just before a delivery ensure:

- The cellar floor is clean
- You have the stock and order sheets ready
- All the current stock is in date order
- All empty containers are ready to return (all casks should be corked with a bung).

## Accepting the delivery

- Check the dates on each one of the containers – every container should have ONE label
- Check the stock is the stock you ordered – is it the beer you require?
- Ensure all kegs have a plastic or foil cap covering the spear
- Make sure there are no leaking containers
- Check the stock matches the delivery note
- Make sure the entrance/drop to the cellar is free from obstruction.

A good tip is to mark up all current stock in the cellar with chalk or a sticker prior to the delivery. This enables you to count the new stock in quickly and accurately

## Best-before dates

It is important that every container has a label so we can check the best-before date. Check that:

- Casks have at least **14** days ahead of the Best Before date
- Kegs have at least **20** days ahead of the Best Before date

### Storing the stock

No containers should be left outside the cellar – either full or empty. Temperature outside the cellar is not controlled therefore you could damage the contents. The empty containers are valuable and subject to theft, so it is important that the delivery lorry removes all empty containers.

If there is no room on the delivery lorry to take away all containers, make sure they are stored in a secure area.

### Manual handling

It needs two people to lift anything heavier than a firkin (9-gallon container), so get assistance if you need to move larger containers around the cellar.

No containers should ever be double stacked, for three reasons:

- The containers are heavy and lifting them this height contravenes manual handling policy

- The containers are unstable when double stacked, and could injure anyone working in the cellar

- Kegs are pressurised containers, and when double stacked the spear of the container below can become eroded. In extreme cases, this can cause the spear to shoot out.

### CASK ALE

### Introduction to cask ale

Cask ale is different to every other category of beer as it is not ready to be served when it is delivered to your club. It needs to be 'conditioned' by you before it is served to the customer.

Cask ale is dispensed on the bar through a 'handpull' or 'handpump'.

- Cask ale is *unfiltered* (meaning it has sediment in) and needs settling time, and

- it is *unpasteurised* (which means it is a fresh product, with a shorter shelf life).

Once the cask is delivered into a cellar it is important to move it as few times as possible. Ideally the cask should immediately be placed onto a stillage or into the area of the cellar from where you will dispense it. It is also important not to move or knock the container once it is on sale, as this could disturb the sediment and it will appear cloudy when dispensed.

Cask ale contains sediment which needs to settle prior to the conditioning process. The sediment settles to the base of the cask aided by a product called finings.

- Finings is a product added to cask ale at the final stages of the production process
- Finings act like a magnet to the sediment in the beer
- Finings attach themselves to the sediment and help the sediment settle in the base of the cask
- Finings will only work a certain number of times which is why it is important to move the cask as few times as possible once it is in the cellar

If there is no space on the stillage when the beer is delivered, roll the cask around the cellar prior to stillaging to redistribute the sediment and activate the finings.

### The Stages of conditioning a cask

| | |
|---|---|
| **Autotilts** | Metal cradles which automatically tilt as cask ale is dispensed |
| **Bungs** | Also known as 'corks'. Inserted into the **keystone** of an empty cask to seal the container. |
| **Cask Conditioning** | Maturing process by which residual sugar in cask ale is converted to alcohol and carbon dioxide when **stillaged** in the cellar. (Also known as secondary fermentation) |
| **CAT Test** | All cask ales should be checked for CLARITY, AROMA and TASTE (CAT) before putting on sale |
| **Cellar Temperature** | Between 11°c and 13°c |
| **Chill Haze** | Cloudiness in cask ale due to precipitation of proteins at low temperatures |
| **Scotches** | Wooden triangles used to wedge casks in place and stabilise the cask. Also known as **'wedges'** and **'chocks'** |
| **Dipstick** | A thin metal calibrated rod used to measure how much beer is left in the cask. Inserted through the hole in the **shive.** |

| | |
|---|---|
| **Filtering Back** | Process by which beer remaining in the pipes after a session is filtered back into the cask. This practice is discouraged – the risk of contamination is high with severe implications. Best practice is 'never filter back to cask' Finings A permitted material added to cask ale to aid settling and clarification |
| **Firkin** | A nine-gallon cask ale container |
| **Fobbing** | Too much foam in the beer. Causes wastage |
| **Gyle Number** | A unique identifying number found on the container label which identifies the production run of the beer |
| **Green Beer** | Cask beer before it is conditioned. Tastes 'harsh' |
| **Hard Peg** | A non-porous peg that keeps carbon dioxide trapped in the cask once conditioning is completed. All casks should be 'hard pegged' after a trading session to keep the beer fresh. (Also known as a **'hard spile'**) |
| **Haze** | Cloudy beer, usually due to dirty beer pipes or beer being on sale for too long (cask beer should be sold within 3 days of being put on sale). |
| **Hop Filter** | A small gauze filter which is placed at the end of the beer pipe before it is connected to the cask. Prevents some sediment passing through the beer pipes |
| **Keystone** | Bung for the hole found at the front flat end of the cask. The keystone is pushed into the cask by the cask tap during **tapping** |
| **Kilderkin** | An 18-gallon cask ale container |
| **Litmus Paper** | A test paper to be used after line cleaning to ensure all traces of line cleaning fluid have been eradicated from the beer pipes |
| **PPE** | Personal Protective Equipment - goggles, gloves, apron |
| **Python** | Insulated beer lines that run from the cooling unit in the cellar up to the bar. The python is an insulating jacket keeping the temperature of the beer in the pipes cold. |
| **Remote Cooler** | Cools beer in the beer pipes to the correct dispense temperature by immersion in a cold-water bath |
| **Shive** | Wooden or plastic bung at the top of the cask with a central core. A **hard peg** is driven through the centre and allows carbon dioxide to escape |

| | |
|---|---|
| **Soft Peg** | Manufactured from porous cane, allows carbon dioxide to escape during cask conditioning (also known as a **'soft spile'**) |
| **Stillage** | A firm support for casks that helps keep them still, allowing sediment to settle evenly across the base of the cask. (Also known as a **'rack'**) |
| **Stillaging** | The process by which **casks** are placed in position on the **stillage** after Delivery. Can be made of metal, wood, or brick |
| **Tapping** | The action of inserting a cask tap into the keystone so the cask can later be connected to the beer pipes for dispense |
| **Tilting** | The action of tilting casks when they are 2/3 full to ensure all beer is dispensed from the cask |
| **Universal Peg** | Semi porous pegs (or **'spiles'**). Can act as a **hard** or **soft** peg depending on how firmly it is inserted into the **shive** |
| **Venting** | The controlled release of carbon dioxide by opening the cask using a **hard peg**, then replacing with a **soft peg** |
| **Yield** | The quantity of beer expected from each container. E.g., if a container contains 72 pints, a 100% yield would mean all 72 pints have been sold. |

### Stillaging

- Draymen should place full casks on empty stillions when they deliver. If not, they should be placed at the back of the stillion so that casks on service are drawn from the front. The cask is lifted onto the stillion and then wedged with wooden wedges called 'scotches' to prevent rolling. The cork and shive should be scrubbed clean as soon as the cask is stillaged.


- Ensure the shive and the keystone are vertically aligned and allow the beer to reach cellar temperature which will take between 24 and 48 hours

Venting

- It is usual to vent the cask on arrival to release any excess $CO_2$ which may have built up due to secondary fermentation. Venting is done through the opening at the top of the waist of the cask, called the 'shive', which is filled with a wooden bung or 'spile'. The shive has a small hole, half bored out, through its centre.

- A venting punch is used to knock this hole completely through. A soft or porous spile is then inserted at once to facilitate the controlled escape of $CO_2$. Using a rubber mallet and a hard spile (or 'peg') punch through the 'tut' in the centre of the shive. In most cases you will hear an escape of gas – $CO_2$. The cask has now started to condition. This is called 'venting'

- Check the soft spile in the top every few hours. Many beers are quite lively (we call this 'brisk conditioning') and some beer may escape from the shive. The soft spile will allow excess $CO_2$ to escape, but if it becomes blocked with beer, the cask will stop conditioning. If this happens replace with a clean soft spile

- When the beer has stopped 'fretting', the soft spile is replaced by a hard spile to retain the rest of the $CO_2$. If bubbles continue to form around the soft spile after wiping, it is not yet time to change it. The time to change is after the bubbles stop forming. Ease the hard spile each day to release any subsequent build-up of pressure. (If a hard spile is left in the shive, the cask is sealed again, and will not condition).

**Tapping**

- Follow brewery instructions concerning when a beer should be tapped. Most beer is tapped as soon as it is quiet. Modern casks have a metal keystone bust around the tap hole into which is inserted a plastic keystone or tapping plug

- Hold the tap in one hand and the mallet in the other. The thread of the tap should be on the side where it will meet the pipe. The other end is placed against the keystone plug. After a couple of feeler strokes, drive the tap home with one sharp blow, pushing the cork, or plug, into the cask

**Connecting the beer for sale**

- Leave the beer to condition for a minimum of **24 hours** and then take a sample of the beer from the cask and check it for *clarity, aroma,* *and taste* (the CAT test). If the beer is fully conditioned and passes the CAT test, put a hard spile in the shive until a free beer line is available. This will seal the beer and keep it fresh until you are ready to serve it.

- When a line becomes free, do the CAT test on the beer again prior to attaching the line. It may have been disturbed causing the beer to appear hazy. Connect the beer pipe to the closed tap and then open the tap for service

- If a beer engine is to be used, ease the spile, but be sure it is tapped in firmly at the end of service

- If $CO_2$ top pressure is used, remove spile and replace with a gas spigot screwed firmly into the vent hole with its pressure release cap screwed down. Ensure gas non-return valve is in position before the $CO_2$ pipe is connected

- Check again (If the beer is clear in the cellar but cloudy at the bar it suggests the beer lines have not been cleaned properly).

- Some pubs have **'auto tilts'** – a metal cradle which tilts the container gradually as the quantity of beer in the cask lowers. If you must manually tilt a cask, make sure it is no less than 2/3 full. You can measure this with a dipstick

- At the end of the trading session, hard spile the beer to keep it fresh. Turn the tap off to prevent 'wash back' from the beer lines (this may disturb the sediment)

## Conditioning a cask using 'extractor rods'

Some clubs may use a different method to condition and dispense the beer from the container. This may be because of lack of space for stillage in the cellar. This is known as a vertical extraction system or the siphon system where the cask is placed in position in the cellar in an upright position.

1. On delivery a 2.5cm (1 inch) wedge should be placed under the cask to tilt the beer away from the keystone. This allows a larger air space for an extractor shank to be driven into the cask through the keystone. Allow the beer to reach cellar temperature, this takes 24 to 48 hours.

2. Using a mallet drive the extractor shank through the keystone. The shank should always have a blank nut fitted to prevent the shank from being damaged.

3. Excess pressure should be vented from the cask by opening the vent valve in slow gradual steps until fully open. The beer is now conditioning.

4. When the excess pressure has been vented, remove the blank nut from the shank and insert a clean extractor rod until it touches the bottom of the cask.

5. Withdraw the tube 2.5cm (1 inch) and lock the rod into position. If the tube was resting at the bottom of the cask, the sediment will be drawn through the rod, resulting in hazy or cloudy beer.

6. When you are ready to serve the beer, open the vent valve to the 'on' position, attach a clean beer line onto the extractor rod, and pull through the beer to the bar. Check a sample of the beer at the bar for clarity, aroma, and taste.

7. When the cask is two thirds full, remove the wedge and place at the opposite side of the cask to tilt the beer towards the keystone. This needs to be done very carefully to avoid disturbing the sediment.

8. At the end of the night, turn the vent valve into a closed position to prevent loss of condition and keep the beer fresh.

**Temperature of cask ales**

Whilst cask beer is kept in a temperature-controlled environment and stored at between 11°c and 13°c, some beer lines are very long and can pick up heat on the way to the bar. Some clubs have a cooling unit fitted in the cellar called an Ale Python Control Unit (APC). This is also sometimes known as an Ale Python Temperature Control Unit (APTC). Most of these are situated on the wall in the cellar, but there are a few floor standing units. This takes chilled water from the remote cooler and blends it with water from the mains supply. This goes inside a python (an insulating jacket) with the ale lines, and it maintains the temperature of the ale all the way to the bar.

A few things to remember about the APC:

- If the water level is low in the APC, or it is switched off, your beer will be warm. It needs to be checked regularly

- There is a thermostat on the APC. This should always read '8'

- If your unit is floor standing, there will be a switch giving you the option of 'water bath' or 'ice bank'. Always ensure this is switched to 'water bath' or your ales will be too cold and develop a 'chill haze'.

# KEG BEERS

## Introduction to keg beers

Keg beers include lagers, stouts (such as Guinness) and nitro-keg beers (such as 'smoothflow). They do not need conditioning in the cellar like cask ales because the brewery removes all the sediment, filters the beer, puts it under gas pressure and pasteurises it. So as soon as this beer reaches cellar temperature it is ready to serve.

## Gases

Keg beers require carbon dioxide ($CO^2$) or mixed gas (nitrogen and carbon dioxide) to push beer out of the pressurised keg through the keg coupler. Gas cylinders are highly pressurised and if connected directly up to a keg container it would be dangerous, so the pressure needs to be reduced to a manageable level before connecting to the keg. This is done through a secondary reducing valve which is fitted by technical services.

There are different colour gas lines for different mixes of gas.

Different colour gas lines:

- Grey pipe – CO2 (used for most lagers and ciders
- Green Pipe – 30% CO2/70% nitrogen (used for Guinness and smoothflow beers)
- White pipe - 60% CO2/40% nitrogen (used for lagers and ciders)
- Blue line – air compressor

It is mandatory that every beer cellar storing gas cylinders should display a Gas Warning Card. This states the regulations concerning $CO^2$ cylinders:

- Secure the cylinders upright with chains or straps when in use
- Spare cylinders should be stored horizontally and wedged up
- The cylinders should be kept away from any heat source
- The cylinders should never be dropped or thrown
- The fittings on the cylinders should not be removed or tampered with

## Properties of $CO^2$/mixed gas

$CO^2$ is odourless, colourless, tasteless, and non-visible.

It can be dangerous because if there is excessive $CO_2$ in the atmosphere it can asphyxiate. The first symptoms you may feel if you are exposed to excessive $CO_2$ is drowsiness, as all the oxygen is being sucked from your lungs.

$CO_2$ is a very heavy gas and lies close to the cellar floor when there is a leak. If you feel excessively tired or drowsy your first instinct is to sit down; by doing this, you are closer to the higher concentration of $CO_2$ and it will affect you more quickly.

There are ways of spotting a CO2 leak. If the gas cylinder becomes very heavily iced up around the shoulder or the base, it is a sign that CO2 is leaking from the cylinder. You may be able to hear the escape of gas – a hissing sound. Cylinders may empty out very quickly and the manager finds they must change the cylinder more frequently. Some cellars have an 'oxygen depletion monitor' fitted just outside the cellar which gives a warning signal if there is excessive CO2 in the cellar. If there are any of these signs, follow these guidelines:

- DO NOT enter the cellar
- Call out technical services
- Warn other colleagues not to enter the cellar
- If possible, ventilate the cellar. Open the doors and delivery hatch

It is recommended that the gas supply is switched off at the cylinder, and to all the pumps at the end of the night for safety purposes.

This has another purpose: if the gas supply is left on when no beer is being dispensed (e.g., overnight), the beer in the container starts to absorb the gas, meaning that the first few pints dispensed at the beginning of the next trading session will 'fob' due to excessive $CO_2$.

**Changing a keg**

A keg needs changing when no beer flows from the tap at the bar. It may splutter, or just dispense foam.

In the cellar check which keg needs to go on next by looking at the label on the container. Make sure the oldest stock is connected first.

Switch off the gas supply to the empty keg. You can check which gas tap it is as it will be situated next to the fob detector which is empty. Disconnect the coupler from the empty keg by lifting the handle and turning the coupler anticlockwise. Guinness couplers are slightly different – they do not need twisting, they slide off. Check the inside of the coupler to make sure it is clean.

Place the coupler over the 'spear', and keeping the handle upright, lock the coupler onto the spear by turning clockwise (or sliding it onto the Guinness spear), then push the handle down. It is now safe to switch the gas back on.

## Fob detectors

All keg beers are fed through fob detectors (they are also known as 'cellar buoys'). These are non-return valves which prevent the beer emptying out of the beer line when the container is empty. If a keg is empty, the chamber on the fob detector will be empty. This now needs re-filling before beer can be dispensed at the bar. Fill the chamber by pushing the button down at the top of the chamber. This is called bleeding the fob detector, and some beer may escape from a wastage pipe on the side of the chamber. This needs to be dispensed into a container, rather than onto the cellar floor.

As soon as the chamber is full, the float (a small ball inside the chamber) needs releasing to 'unblock' the flow of beer. At the bottom of the chamber is a button, press this in, then pull out again. You will notice the ball floats to the top of the chamber. The beer is now ready to dispense.

## Coolers

When keg beer is delivered it still needs 1-2 days to reach cellar temperature – 11 to 13°c. However, we want to dispense these beers at a much cooler temperature than the cellar, typically 1 - 8°c. We do this by feeding the keg beer lines through a piece of equipment called a 'remote cooler'. This is a large metal box which contains a bath of liquid consisting of water or a mix of glycol (food grade anti-freeze) and water.

If the remote cooler is just filled with water, it should have an 'ice bank' surrounding the bath of water. All remote coolers have an 'inspection hatch' in the top, and you can feel for this ice bank by putting your fingers just inside the inspection hatch. To maintain this ice bank, the cooler needs to be topped up with water regularly. If there is no water in the cooler, the ice bank melts, and beer temperatures will rise, and the beer will froth when dispensed.

It is also important to make sure there is nothing blocking the vents around the base of the cooler, so do not stack containers, or bag in boxes around the vents.

Glycol coolers enable the beer to reach 'super-chilled' temperatures of 1°c - 3°c in the most efficient and consistent way. However, only technical services should top the cooler up with the mix of glycol and water.

Python

When the keg beer lines emerge from the cooler they are fed through a 'python'. A python has two wide bore lines which take a supply of chilled water from the cooler and circulate it inside an insulating jacket all the way to the bar, and then back down to the cooler. The keg beer lines 'hug' the cold-water lines inside the insulating jacket, which helps maintain the temperature of the beer all the way to the dispense point.

## LINE CLEANING AND CHEMICALS

### Introduction to beer-line cleaning

If all the beer lines are not cleaned every seven days, yeast builds up in the lines and causes:

- Haziness

- Fobbing

- 'Off' flavours

- 'Off' aromas

Customers will bring beer back if it is served in this condition and yields and profitability will be severely affected. Use a brewery recommended line cleaning product.

### The line cleaning process

### Keg ales

- Detach connectors from kegs and connect to ring main and shut off gas to connectors

- Supply clean, cold water to ring main and flush out beer at taps on the bar until all the beer is removed and clean water is pulled through

- Line cleaner and water is then supplied into the ring main and drawn through at the taps

- Leave for one hour

- Flush cold water through the ring main and rinse – at least a gallon per tap
- Check for clarity and smell – line cleaner has a 'soapy' consistency and smells of bleach
- Clean connectors and re-connect beer barrels and draw beer through at the taps, sample for clarity, taste, and smell
- Leave clean water in disused lines

## Cask ales

- Same procedure as for kegs, except lines must be cleaned individually and not via a ring main.

## COSHH: Control of Substances Hazardous to Health (see Section 9 Health and Safety)

Beer line cleaner is one of most caustic substances we keep at a club, so a system of rules is in place to reduce risks when handling the product. These rules are called: COSHH,

COSHH is a system implemented in all industries to eliminate and eradicate risks when handling chemicals.

It is a legal requirement that all staff involved in the handling and use of chemicals are aware of risks and follow instructions:

- Always wear Personal Protective Equipment (PPE). These can be found in the cellar tidy, and as a minimum include goggles, gloves, and an apron
- Store cleaning detergents in a safe place, preferably a locked or secure cupboard. They should not be stored on the cellar floor
- Do not mix any chemicals, or decant chemicals into other containers
- Read the dosage instructions on the side of the container. Use a measuring vessel to accurately measure the precise amount of detergent required
- Use litmus/test paper to check all line cleaning detergent has been eradicated from the beer lines, before serving the beer

## 7.0    How to Deliver the Perfect Serve

### Introduction

The purpose of this 'How To' guide is to provide a basic instruction manual for bar stewards in how to prepare and serve beverage alcohol and soft drinks' products legally and in a manner that offers the product in premium condition for consumption by the customer – hence the term 'perfect serve'. It can also be used as a training manual for bar staff. Even though clubs are run by volunteers, it is important that the service of all drinks is done legally, hygienically, and professionally if customers' expectations are to be met.

This manual will also assist club committees understand what standards they and their members should expect when serving drinks' products.

| Legal measures for draught lager, cask ale and keg beer | The legal units of measurement that can be used for the dispense of draught lager and beer products and the types of glasses that can be used for dispense: |
|---|---|
| **Narrative** A ⅓ of a pint is rarely used as a measure. It is sometimes used for very strong ciders and beers and the measure is referred to as a 'nip'. Most lagers, ales and keg beers are therefore sold in ½ pint or pint glasses. 2/3 measures – 'Schooners' are now legal. Tip: Schooners are 2/3 of a pint but offer better margin - usually sold for 70% of the price of a pint. | • All forms of lager, cider, ale, and beer, when dispensed on draught can only be dispensed in measures of a ⅓ of a pint, 2/3 of a pint, ½ a pint or multiples of ½ a pint |
|  | • Where the dispense is from a free-flow delivery system into a brim measure glass the beer must constitute 95% of the content and head no more than 5% (always give a top-up if asked) |
| A free-flow beer delivery system means one where the server uses a tap or hand-pull and thereby determines how much beer is poured. A metered system involved pressing a button that generates the delivery of a pre-measured or 'metered' amount of beer – ½ pint or pint. Cask ale and Guinness are never delivered through metered delivery systems – only lagers and keg beers. | • Where the dispense is from a metered delivery system a lined, oversized glass will be used and the head will be additional to the liquid beer |
|  | • Brim measure glasses must be Government stamped – a small white Crown on the glass |
|  | • Lined, oversized glasses do not need to be Government stamped because the meter itself is. |
|  | • It is as much of an offence to sell over-measure as to sell under-measure |

| Lager – perfect serve, preparation | The steps involved in preparing to serve lager:<br>• Ensure the correct sparkler is attached to the tap<br>• Ensure the nozzle is clean and has been cleaned in sanitizer<br>• Check the beer temperature every day before service – should be between $1 – 8°C$<br>• Ensure the bar is well stocked with clean, cool, branded glassware<br>• Ensure the font or T-bar is spotlessly clean |
|---|---|
| Understanding lager | The key facts about lager:<br>• Lager is filtered and pasteurised at the brewery and arrives ready for sale<br>• It has a longer shelf life than cask conditioned ale (see sell-by date label on barrel)<br>• Essential to serve in a branded glass because lager glasses are 'nucleated' – the etching or logo on the glass aggravated the $CO_2$ in the liquid ensuring the beer retains its head |
| Lager – the perfect serve | The elements of a perfect serve of lager:<br>• Serve in a dry, clean, cold branded glass<br>• Hold the glass at a 45° angle with your fingers around the bottom half of the glass<br>• Open the tap fully towards you<br>• Pour the beer aimed at the logo ensuring the beer creates the right amount of head<br>• Straighten the glass during the pour once the right amount of head is formed<br>• Close the tap when the glass is full<br>• Present to the customer with the logo facing forward |

## Cask ale and keg beers

| Cask ale – preparation | The steps involved in preparing to serve cask ale:<br>• Taste the product to detect whether the beer is 'off' – tasting of vinegar or yeast<br>• Ensure that the pump clip is attached and facing towards the customer<br>• Ensure the brassware is spotlessly clean<br>• Ensure the bar is well stocked with clean, cold, dry glasses (branded if possible) |
|---|---|

| Understanding the product | Key facts about cask ale: |
|---|---|
| | • Cask ale is conditioned in the cellar |
| | • Is unfiltered, unpasteurised and needs time to settle before it is ready for sale |
| | • It can be on sale for up to 3 days – after which the condition of the beer begins to deteriorate due to exposure to the air |
| | • It is served at between 11 and 13°C |
| | • Cask ale is poured through two different types of spout: |
| | ➢ 'long spouts' – which usually have a sparkler (nozzle) attached to create a thicker creamier head |
| | ➢ 'short spouts' – do not use sparklers - this creates a looser, more foamy head |
| Long spout: the perfect serve | The elements of a 'perfect serve' of cask ale using the long spout: |
| | • Cool, clean dry glass |
| | • Hold the glass around the bottom half |
| | • With the glass held straight, place the sparkler at the base of the glass and keeping it there pull the handpull towards you firmly in one pull |
| | • Still keeping the sparkler at the base of the glass push the handpull back fully and repeat the action |
| | • As the beer reaches the rim of the glass, draw the glass away from the spout, keeping the sparkler underneath the surface of the beer always |
| | • Let the beer settle if necessary and then top up |
| | • Present to the customer with branding facing them |
| Short spout: the perfect serve | The elements of a 'perfect serve' of cask ale using the short spout: |
| | • Cool, clean, dry glass |
| | • Hold the glass around the bottom half |
| | • With the glass held at 45° angle, insert the spout into the glass, remembering not to touch the glass with the spout |
| | • Pull the handpull towards you firmly and in one pull |
| | • Push the handpull back and repeat the action |
| | • Ensure the spout does not go into the beer as it rises up the glass |

| | |
|---|---|
| | • As the glass fills start straightening the glass until it is brimful<br>• Let the beer settle if necessary and then top up<br>• Present to the customer with branding facing them |
| **Keg ale - preparation** | The steps involved in preparing to serve Keg ale:<br>• Ensure the bar is well stocked with clean, cold, dry glasses (branded if possible)<br>• Ensure the correct nozzle is attached to the tap<br>• Ensure the font is spotlessly clean |
| Understanding the product | The key facts about keg ale:<br>• The majority of keg ale is referred to as 'smooth' or 'creamflow'. The gas used to dispense these beers ensures a creamy 'tight' head<br>• Keg ale is filtered and pasteurised at the brewery<br>• It has a longer shelf life than cask ale<br>• It is served colder than cask ale – usually at between 5 and 8°C |
| Keg ale – the perfect serve | The elements of a 'perfect serve' of keg ale:<br>• Clean, cool, dry glass<br>• Hold the glass around the bottom half<br>• With the glass held at 45° angle, insert the spout into the glass<br>• Remember not to touch the glass with the nozzle<br>• Open the tap fully towards you and pour the beer down the side of the glass<br>• As the glass fills start straightening the glass until it is brimful<br>• Let the beer settle if necessary, then top up<br>• Present to the customer with branding facing towards them |

## Guinness and other stouts

| | |
|---|---|
| Guinness or other stouts – preparation for service | How to prepare Guinness for serving to ensure a consistent quality serve each time:<br>• Ensure that lines and nozzles are cleaned regularly<br>• Ensure that Guinness is not past its sell-by date<br>• Check the product tastes right<br>• Ensure well stocked with branded glasses |

| Glassware | The types of glasses that should be used for serving Guinness:<br>• Pint and half pint tulip glasses<br>• Correctly branded for Original, Extra Cold and Red<br>• Ensure glasses are clean and cold |
|---|---|
| Guinness - the perfect serve | The steps involved in pouring a pint of Guinness:<br>• Clean, cool, branded tulip glass<br>• Two part pour lasting 119.3 seconds<br>• 1st part: hold glass at 45° angle, pour until ¾ full; allow to surge and settle – place on bar with branding facing customer; tilt tap away from you to fill to the top; present to customer with branding facing towards them<br>Understand that:<br>• The two-part pour is integral to serving Guinness correctly<br>• It is part of the Guinness experience that cannot be replicated at home<br>• It demonstrates that you understand and appreciate the product<br>• Guinness has many enthusiasts who would reject your club if poured incorrectly<br>• You are adding value to their experience |

## Spirits and mixers

| Preparation | The most important elements of preparing a bar for service of spirits and mixers:<br>• A well-stocked bar<br>• Full ice buckets<br>• Early preparation of garnishes<br>• Maintaining a good supply of correct, clean glasses<br>• Maintaining a sufficient supply of mixers<br>And this is important to ensure:<br>• The provision of efficient and effective service<br>• Freedom to interact with customers<br>• The provision of a consistently high-quality serve |
|---|---|
| Glassware | Glassware basics:<br>• The importance of clean, cool glassware<br>• Which types of spirits glasses to use:<br>➢ the 12oz Highball/Slim Jim/Collins for the core spirits for long spirits and a mixer (refer to the manager which type should be used) |

| | |
|---|---|
| | ➤ Single serve spirits and Baileys – tumbler/rocks glass<br>➤ Balloon or 'snifter' glass for brandy when served as a stand-alone drink (technically a distilled wine)<br>➤ Sherries and liqueurs should be served in a schooner<br><br>• Correct and cool glassware enhances the drink<br>• That customers will notice dirty glassware<br>• That correct, cool and clean glassware impacts on the customers perception of the quality of the outlet |
| Measure size<br><br>**Narrative**<br>Operators must decide which measure to use – 25 ml or 35 ml – it is one or the other, they cannot be mixed in the same licensed premises.<br>The single measure must be available.<br><br>These measures are only a legal requirement for the 'core spirits' – whisky, gin, rum (Navy and white) and vodka. There are no measures expressly required by law for other spirits or liqueurs or fortified wines like Martini, but measures expressed on price lists must be metric measures.<br><br>These measures do not apply when a drink including the core spirits contains 3 or more liquids, e.g., cocktails. | The two spirit measure sizes allowed under Weights & Measures legislation:<br>• 25 ml and 35 ml or multiples thereof - and whether to serve 'singles' or 'doubles' but whichever measure is chosen it must be available as a single measure "smaller sizes".<br>It is important to offer customers a choice of single or double.<br>Calculate the number of units in each drink based on the following formula:<br>Quantity of liquid x % ABV x 0.001 = units of alcohol.<br>e.g., 25 ml whisky x 40% ABV x 0.001 = 1 unit |
| Understanding your spirits | The core spirits:<br>• whisky, gin, dark and white rum, vodka<br>• Brandy is a distilled wine but treated as a spirit<br>• Martinis, sherry, and port are fortified wines |

| | Identify spirit and mixer combinations: |
|---|---|
| | • Spirits may be mixed with a variety of mixers or fruit juices. Traditionally the following go together: |
| | ➢ Whisky and water, or whisky and dry ginger/coke |
| | ➢ Gin and tonic |
| | ➢ Bacardi (white rum) and cola |
| | ➢ Dark rum (Navy rum) and cola |
| | ➢ Vodka and coke or a variety of fruit juices, e.g. orange |
| | ➢ Brandy, when not served as a stand-alone drink would be mixed with coke in a 12oz Highball glass |
| Upselling | What questions to ask to make the most of each sale: |
| | • If the brand the customer wants is not available, offer an alternative |
| | • Ask "single or double?" |
| | • Ask what mixer the customer wants |
| | • Ask "can I offer you anything else?" |
| | Understand the reasons for a positive upselling effort: |
| | • The customer is more confident in buying a drink from a knowledgeable seller |
| | • The club will make more money |
| | • Prompting the customer reminds them of purchases they might have forgotten, e.g., mixers |
| The serve | What constitutes the 'perfect serve'? |
| | • Always use the appropriate, clean, cool glass |
| | • Fill at ¾ with ice (if the drink requires ice) |
| | • Pour spirit measure over the ice |
| | • Add all mixer, unless the customer states otherwise |
| | • Add correct garnish and straw (where appropriate) |
| | • Present to customer on Bevan |
| | Understand why providing the perfect serve is important: |
| | • It improves the taste and longevity of the drink |
| | • It demonstrates your expertise and product knowledge |
| | • It makes the customer feel that valued |
| | • It improves customer perception of the quality and value for money of your outlet |

# Wines

| Understanding your wine list | The importance of a basic knowledge of your outlets wine list: |
|---|---|
| **Narrative** We do not expect bar staff to be wine experts, but customers sometimes ask for advice. Know your product range. 68% of the UK adult population drink wine and wine is now the biggest alcohol drinks' category by value in the UK. Be aware also that customers sometimes order wine by grape variety, or 'varietal' - 70% of on-trade consumers choose their wine by grape variety. The most popular are Pinot Gigi and Chardonnay (white) and Merlot and Shiraz (red).  This information should be on the wine bottle label or price list. | • Learn which wines are the most popular on your club's wine list • Taste the wines on your list • Know where to get information to give simple, positive descriptions of each wine – this information is frequently found on the wine list or bottle • Be able to advise on food/wine combinations – this information is frequently found on the bottle or wine list • Be able to make knowledgeable recommendations • If unsure about a customer query or how to advise, escalate the query to your manager |
| Wine storage | Know how different types of wine should be stored: • White and rose wines kept in cooler • Red wines not kept in cooler • Clean and dry • Corked bottles laid on their sides, label up • When a bottle of wine has been opened for service by the glass, put the cork or cap back in between service • Rotate stocks – first in, first out Understand the reasons for good storage: • Maintenance of quality • Temperature changes can spoil wine; heat and light will prematurely age it • Corks will dry out if not kept moist, allowing air into the bottle • Wine is delivered ready for drinking and will not benefit from time in storage |

| Service temperature | The correct temperatures at which different wines should be served: |
|---|---|
| | • White and rose wine: 8 -10°C, not too cold |
| | • Red wine: 15 - 18°C, not too warm |
| | • Sparkling wine: 6 - 8°C |
| | Understand how serving wine at the wrong temperature impacts on quality: |
| | • Chilling wine subdues flavour and acidity, thus enhancing the freshness of white and rose wines |
| | • Red wines lose their fruit and become 'flabby' if served too warm |
| Glassware | Identify the types of glasses that should be used for serving wines: |
| | • Tulip shaped and of sufficient size |
| | • Larger glasses are traditionally used for red wine |
| | • Glasses must be spotlessly clean and polished |
| Measure size<br><br>**Narrative**<br>Unlike the case with spirit measures, both measures of wine by the glass, and some or all of the quantities of wine sold by carafe can be used on the same premises, but the price list must set out which quantities are in use and the small measure must be available. | Identify the different measures of wine by the glass, the carafe and bottle: |
| | • Weights & Measures law states wine by the glass must be sold in measures of |
| | - 125 ml |
| | - 175 ml |
| | Or multiples of these quantities. Customers should be offered a choice. |
| | • If sold by the carafe: |
| | - 25, 50, 75 class and 1 litre |
| | • If sold by the bottle: |
| | - Baby bottles 187 ml or 250 ml |
| | • Offer the customer a choice of measures |
| The serve | State how to serve wine from the bottle in such a way as to make the customer confident he is getting the wine ordered. Ideally the server should: |
| | • Present the bottle to the customer |
| | • Pour from the bottle in front of the customer |
| | • Use a measure if glasses not lined |
| | • Where bag in box or draught wine is used dispense into a lined glass |
| Wine faults | Recognise potential wine faults and the reasons for them: |
| | • Corked wine – musty smell like wet cardboard |
| | - Corks are not all perfect and can cause faults |

| | |
|---|---|
| | • Oxidised wine – vinegary and dried out<br>   - Once spoiled a wine is not drinkable<br>• Sediment – tartrates are harmless but look bad<br>   - Customer must be satisfied with the wine served – open another bottle if necessary |

## Soft drinks

| | |
|---|---|
| Coca-Cola (bottled): storage | The importance of chilled storage and stock rotation:<br>• Store away from sunlight and chilled on the bar in a fridge at between 3 and 5°C<br>• Rotate stock on a 'sell-by' date basis. |
| Bottled Coca-Cola: the perfect serve (when served straight) | Identify the importance of making the service of Coca-Cola 'special':<br>• Fill 1/3 of glass with ice<br>• Pour in correctly chilled Coca-Cola<br>• Add appropriate, fresh garnish – to 'make it special'<br>• Ensure the label is facing the customer when you pour |
| Glassware | The importance of using the correct glassware:<br>• Use the branded 16oz Georgia Green Coca-Cola glass |
| Marketing & Merchandising | The importance of stocking the fridge correctly:<br>• 'Eye-level is buy-level' – make sure the fridge is at eye level<br>• The top left corner sells more products because customers 'read' fridges from left to right and top to bottom – so most popular products in top left corner<br>• Fridges should be kept full and new stock added to the back of the fridge so that you only sell chilled stock<br>• All bottles should be clean and have labels facing the front<br>• Place brands together in the fridge |
| Coca-Cola and lemonade post mix: the perfect serve | The elements of the perfect serve of post mix products:<br>• Always draw at least 1 pint of carbonated water through before serving any product<br>• At the end of a session clean dispense valves with a brush and warm water using the supplied Make it special cleaning kit |

| | • Check the temperature is at 5°C or below |
| | • Remember 4 key points: |
| | 1. Carbonation – flat products affects the quality of the drink |
| | 2. Ratio – too little syrup means you are serving an inferior product |
| | 3. Temperature – must be sold at 5°C or below |
| | 4. Hygiene – dirty equipment is a health hazard |
| Mixers and fruit juices as stand-alone drinks – the serve | State the importance of correct service procedure: <br> • Take a tall, cool glass filled 2/3 full with ice and use the appropriate garnish |

## Coffee

| Different styles of coffee <br><br> **Narrative** <br> There are other styles of coffee that you might typically find in a specialist high street coffee shop, but the ones mentioned here are the most common styles sold in pubs. | The different styles of coffee: <br> • Espresso <br> • Cafe Latte (with steamed milk and milk foam) <br> • Flat White (with steamed milk) <br> • Café Brave (with milk foam and steamed half and half) <br> • Cappuccino (with steamed milk and milk foam 50/50) <br> • Americano (Espresso with water) <br> • Filtered coffee – not poured through an espresso machine but filtered into a glass coffee decanter |
| Serving coffee <br><br> **Narrative** <br> Using an espresso machine safely and effectively requires training. This should be provided by your manager or the supplier of the machine. | Deliver the same coffee service standards as those found on the high street: <br> • Always use a clean, warm cup <br> • Ideally, offer skimmed or semi-skimmed milk, sugar, and optional biscuits <br> • Keep fresh coffee beans in the fridge <br> • Maintain a clean machine |

## 8.0 How to Comply with Food Allergens Law

## FOOD ALLERGENS

### Introduction

Most Conservative clubs have a food offer. In addition to understanding basic food hygiene it is important that staff engaged in preparing, cooking, taking orders and serving food to members and guests in your club have an awareness of food allergens and intolerances. The content of this booklet will raise awareness of food allergens and intolerances as well as providing an overview of the law. This will assist club staff in advising diners who may have food allergies or intolerances. There have been numerous high-profile cases in recent years of tragedies arising out of incorrect information, or lack of information, given to diners with food allergies.

## Rules and legislation

### Allergen rules

On the 13th December 2014, the EU Food Information for Consumers Regulation came into force. This required a change to the way in which allergen information appears on food labels and food sold loose or served out of home.

You will also need to be able to answer any consumer questions regarding 'allergenic ingredients' contained in the food you serve.

An allergenic ingredient in any food is an ingredient that can cause an allergic reaction in a person who suffers from an allergy to that particular ingredient.

The EU Food Information for Consumers Regulation outlines 14 allergens (and products of them) that must be labelled or indicated as being present in foods. These are:

- Eggs
- Milk (including lactose)
- Shellfish, e.g., prawns, crabs, lobster, crayfish
- Mollusc, e.g., clams, mussels, whelks, oysters, snails, and squid
- Fish
- Peanuts
- Sesame seeds
- Soybeans
- Sulphur dioxide
- Nuts such as almonds, hazelnuts, walnuts, cashews, pecan nuts, Brazil nuts, pistachio nuts, macadamia (or Queensland) nuts
- Cereals containing gluten such as wheat, rye, barley, oats, spelt or khorasan
- Celery (including celeriac)
- Mustard
- Lupin

A food label must use a typeset that clearly distinguishes information about allergenic ingredients from the other ingredients in a food product. If you are operating a retail food business, you should check for the presence of correct information on the label.

Where a product is not required to give a list of ingredients, if there are any allergenic ingredients within the product, they must be declared using a 'contains' statement followed by the name or names of the allergenic ingredients concerned.

Where several ingredients or processing aids in a food originate from a single allergenic ingredient, the labelling should make this clear for each ingredient or processing aid concerned, e.g., skimmed **milk** powder, whey **(milk)**, lactose **(milk)**.

Where the name of the food (such as a box of eggs or bag of peanuts) clearly refers to the allergenic ingredients concerned, there is no need for a separate declaration of the allergenic food.

Where foods are offered for sale to the final consumer or to mass caterers without packaging, or where foods are packed on the sales premises at the consumer's request, or pre-packed for direct sale, information about allergenic ingredients is mandatory and must be provided.

Allergen information must be provided for non-pre-packed foods in written or oral formats with clear signposting to where consumers can obtain this information, when it is not provided upfront in a written format.

### Applicable law

In addition to the criminal law regime that governs food labelling, liability can also arise under civil law. The applicable law is the Consumer Protection Act 1987; civil liability also arises under the common law of negligence.

### Important definitions

The new allergen consumer information requirements apply to all mass caterers or catering establishments. The following definitions are to assist in identifying what type of establishments are covered by the regulations and what the terminology means in relation to how food is sold:

**Catering establishments** – means retail catering businesses of all types where, during business, food is prepared for delivery to the person or people consuming it and which is ready for consumption without further preparation. Such premises include:

- Social clubs

- Restaurants and cafes

- Clubs, pubs, and bars

- Canteens, schools and hospitals or care establishments

Pre-packed or loose foods

**Pre-packed food -** means foods which have been packaged before they are sold – either to    caterers for retail sale, or to consumers    where there's no opportunity for direct communication between the producer and the customer, and the contents cannot be altered without opening the package or changing it. Examples include ready-made meals, tinned foods and frozen food products sold from convenience stores and supermarkets.

**Pre-packed for direct sale -** means those foods that have been pre-packed at the premises as they are being sold. Generally, these foods do not have to be labelled, because there is an opportunity for the customer to ask staff who pre-packed or made the foods about their ingredients. Examples would include sandwiches or meat pies and pasties made on-site and sold either pre-packed, or not pre-packed from the premises where they were made.

**Non-pre–packed -** means foods sold from retail premises such as cheese, pizza, pies, fish; or food sold from bakery shops such as bread. In catering establishments this would include meals served for immediate consumption in restaurants or cafes or similar premises.

## Criminal law

The current food labelling rules were introduced by European Directive 2000/13/EC and have subsequently been amended by Directives 2003/89/EC and 2007/68/EC.

The purpose of these Directives is to ensure that consumers are given information about the use of allergenic ingredients in food products. This is particularly important for people with food allergies as it enables them to identify which foods they need to avoid.

The new allergen labelling rules apply to England, Scotland, Wales, and Northern Ireland. They replace several rules and laws that apply up to the 12th December 2014. From the 13th December 2014 the EU Food Information for Consumers (EU FIC) Regulation applies. The regulations under this directive require the declaration of the specified allergenic foods when they are used as ingredients in:

- Pre-packed foods

- Foods pre-packed for direct sale, and

- Non-pre-packed foods

The regulations do not cover accidental cross-contamination of a product with any allergenic food ingredients listed under the new regulations. There is other law that may be applicable to this issue.

## Civil law

Under the Consumer Protection Act 1987 a manufacturer may be liable under civil law for supplying defective food products. A manufacturer can be held liable for injury, loss or damage suffered by a consumer because of such supply, regardless of whether there is evidence of negligence.

Under common law manufacturers owe a 'duty of care' to their consumers to only supply safe products. Discharging that duty requires them to take all reasonable steps to ensure the safety of their products. Clearly, labelling those products with any allergenic ingredients they contain is a reasonable step as well as a statutory requirement. If there are allergenic ingredients that are unintentionally present in a food product they will obviously not be labelled as ingredients.

Under the Consumer Protection Act 1987 a product that is unintentionally cross contaminated with an allergen may be defective. It is unclear about whether an advisory statement to the effect that cross-contamination may have taken place will cover the manufacturer against legal action. Clearly, if other manufacturers are providing information about the possibility of cross-contamination then a manufacturer that does not do so would be in some difficulty in establishing a due diligence defence.

### Allergies and their effects in the body

### Definition of a food allergy

**Food allergy** – occurs when the body's immune system mistakenly attacks a food protein.

**Allergic reactions** – to foods can vary in severity but can be potentially fatal.

### Symptoms of an allergic reaction

There are many different physical reactions that can occur when a person is exposed to an allergen. The type of reaction and the severity of it are very individual and depend on the severity of the allergy. The severity of an allergic reaction does not necessarily depend on the amount of the allergen the individual is exposed to. Even small amounts of some allergens, such as nuts, can cause severe adverse reactions.

These can include:

- Faintness
- Collapse
- Anaphylactic shock (this can be fatal)

Below are some common physical reactions:

| BODY PART | PHYSICAL REACTION |
|---|---|
| Eyes | Sore, red, and/or itchy |
| Nose | Runny, and/or blocked |
| Lips | Swelling of the lips |
| Throat | Coughing, dry, itchy, and swollen throat |
| Chest | Coughing, wheezing and shortness of breath |
| Gut | Nausea and feeling bloated; diarrhoea |
| Skin | Itchy, and/or a rash |

The above information is not a comprehensive description of allergic reactions but indicates the serious consequences that can occur if customers are exposed to allergens. Staff working in restaurants, pubs and bars or similar premises need to be able to recognise common symptoms if they are to respond appropriately to their customers' needs.

**Definition of food intolerance**

A 'food intolerance' is not the same thing as a food allergy. Food intolerance is the body's inability to digest a particular food. A common type of food intolerance is lactose intolerance.

**Symptoms of food intolerance**

- Abdominal cramps
- Bloating
- Diarrhoea

Club restaurants should provide consumers with accurate information about ingredients so that they can make informed decisions about what to order.

## Definition of anaphylactic reaction

An anaphylactic reaction is a potentially life-threatening allergic reaction suffered by people with severe food allergies.

## Symptoms of an anaphylactic reaction

- A drop in blood pressure
- Loss of consciousness
- Can lead to death

An anaphylactic reaction is a medical emergency and if a consumer is suffering an anaphylactic reaction you should call emergency services and get medical assistance immediately.

## Allergen descriptions

| ALLERGEN | ALLERGEN DESCRIPTION |
|---|---|
| **EGG**<br>Includes all food products that contain egg and egg derivatives.<br><br>Other names for egg: albumin, egg (dried, powdered, solids, white, yolk).<br><br>Food and food products that contain or may contain egg: meringue, mayonnaise, pasta, creamy sauces, and salad dressings, e.g., tartare, hollandaise, and baked goods. | Egg allergy is a hypersensitivity to dietary substances from the yolk or white of eggs, causing an over-reaction of the immune system. |
| **MILK**<br>All food products that contain milk and milk derivatives.<br><br>Other names for milk: casein, whey, lactose, milk protein<br><br>Food and food products that may contain milk: milk powder, buttermilk, yoghurt, cream, ice cream, cheese, curds, custards, butter, ghee and butter fat, margarine. | A milk allergy is an adverse immune reaction to one or more of the constituents of milk from any animal. |

| | |
|---|---|
| **SHELLFISH AND MOLLUSCS**<br>Other names for shellfish: shrimp (crevette), prawns, crab, crayfish, and lobster. Other names for molluscs: clams, cockles, mussels, octopus, oysters, snails, squid (calamari), and scallops. | Food allergy to shellfish is quite common and is one of the most frequent triggers of anaphylactic reactions. Allergy to molluscs has been reported less frequently. Shellfish and molluscs contain the same type of proteins, so some people may react to both. |
| **FISH**<br>All foods and products that contain fish and fish derivatives. Cod, salmon, and tuna are the fish that have been most studied in respect of allergies.<br><br>Food and food products that contain or may contain fish: ethnic dishes such as paella, spring rolls and fried rice; salad dressings and sauces, e.g., seafood soups, soy, and barbeque sauce. | More than half of all people who are allergic to one type of fish are allergic to other fish. People with a fish allergy would be well-advised to avoid eating all fish.<br><br>Finned fish can cause severe allergic reactions and is usually a life-long allergy. |
| **PEANUTS**<br>All foods and food products that contain peanuts or ingredients derived from peanuts.<br><br>Other names for peanuts: ground nuts, beer nuts, monkey nuts, arachis oil, kernels, mandelonas, peanut protein.<br><br>Food and food products that may contain peanuts: ethnic dishes such as African, Asian, and Mexican; vegetarian meat substitutes, hydrolysed plant or vegetable protein, sauces and dressings, (e.g., chilli, pesto, gravy, mole, enchilada, satay) and sweets and cereals. | Peanut allergy is a hypersensitive reaction to dietary substances from peanuts that causes an over-reaction of the immune system. It is a different kind of allergic reaction to that caused by tree nuts. |
| **SOY**<br>All food and food products that contain soy or ingredients derived from soy.<br><br>Other names for soy: soya, soybean, soy protein, textured vegetable protein, endamame, bean curd, tofu, soy lecithin.<br><br>Food and food products that contain or may contain soy: soybean butter, soy milk, soy oil, hydrolysed vegetable, plat, or soy protein sauces (e.g., teriyaki), miso, cereals, and vegetarian dishes. | Soy allergy is a hypersensitivity to dietary substances from soy causing an over-reaction of the immune system. Symptoms are usually mild although it has been known to cause anaphylaxis. |

| | |
|---|---|
| **SESAME**<br>All food and food products that contain sesame and or ingredients derived from sesame.<br><br>Other names for sesame: benne (benne seed, benniseed), gingelly.<br><br>Food and food products that contain or may contain sesame: sesame oil, brad, crackers, cereals, dips, (e.g., hummus), ethnic foods (e.g., stews and stir fries) and tahini paste. | Sesame allergy is a hypersensitivity to dietary substances from sesame seeds causing an over-reaction of the immune system. |
| **SULPHUR DIOXIDE**<br>All food and food products that contain sulphur dioxide and its derivatives.<br><br>Other names for sulphur dioxide: potassium bisulphite or metabisulphite, sodium bisulphite, dithionite, metabisulphite or sulphite. E220-228 (European additive numbers) | Sulphur dioxide can cause symptoms similar to an allergy in people with asthma and allergic rhinitis. The most common reaction is wheezing, tight chest and cough, which can be sever and distressing. |
| **NUTS**<br>Includes almonds, hazelnuts, walnuts, cashews, pecan nuts, Brazil nuts, pistachio nuts, macadamia (or Queensland) nuts.<br><br>Food and food products that contain or may contain nuts: tree nut oil, marzipan, nougat, nut extracts, paste or butters, chocolate and chocolate spreads, ethnic and vegetarian dishes, salads and dressings, marinades, mortadella (may contain pistachios), cereals and crackers. | Nut allergy is a hypersensitivity to dietary substances from tree nuts causing an over-reaction of the immune system which can lead to severe symptoms. Most people with an allergy to tree nuts tend to have a lifelong allergy. |
| **CEREALS CONTAINING GLUTEN**<br>All foods and food products derived from or containing wheat (all forms, including durum, semolina, spelt, kamut, wincorn and faro), barley rye, oat, malt, couscous.<br><br>Food or food products that contain or may contain: bread, baked goods, baking mixes, pasta, breadcrumbs, crackers, beer, malt coffee, muesli mixes, gluten-based additives, spreads, seasonings and condiments, sauces, chocolate bars, drinks containing cocoa, surimi, hydrolysed wheat protein. | Gluten intolerance is caused by the body's inability to break down gluten, which is a protein in wheat and other grains. Gluten intolerance can cause a digestive condition called Coeliac disease. Sufferers must eliminate gluten from their diet. |

| | |
|---|---|
| **CELERY AND CELERIAC**<br>Other names for celery and celery-products: celery stalk, celery leaf, celeriac, and celery seed.<br><br>Food or food products that contain or may contain celery: celery salt, vegetable juices containing celery, spice mixes, curry, bouillons, soups, stews, sauces, processed meat products, sausages, salads such as Waldorf salad, vegetable salad, potato salad with bouillon, savoury snacks. | Allergy to celeriac, which is the celery root, is more common than the celery stick. Both can cause severe reactions, from mild ones such as oral allergy syndrome to anaphylactic shock |
| **MUSTARD**<br>Other names for mustard and mustard products: mustard seed, mustard leaves, mustard flower, mustard oil, sprouted mustard seeds, mustard powder.<br><br>Food or food products that contain or may contain mustard: sausages, processed meat products, roulade, spice mixes, pickles, marinades, soups, sauces, chutneys, delicatessen salad, some mayonnaises, barbecue sauce, fish paste, ketchup, tomato sauce, piccalilli, pizza, salad dressings, Indian food including curries | The symptoms of mustard allergy may come on rapidly, usually within minutes, but sometimes up to two hours. |
| **LUPIN**<br>Other names for lupin and its products: lupine, lupin flour, lupin seed, lupin bean.<br><br>Food products that contain or may contain lupin: lupin flour, lupin seed, lupin bean, baked goods such as pastries, pies, waffles, pancakes, pasta products, pizzas, vegetarian meat substitutes, lupin sprouts | Cases of lupin allergy in the UK are rare because lupin is not a typical ingredient of foods in the UK.<br>In mainland Europe lupin flour is commonly used in food products and lupin allergies are much more common there as a result. |
| **LACTOSE INTOLERANCE**<br>All food or food products that contain lactose, such as milk and dairy products may cause symptoms in people who suffer lactose intolerance.<br><br>Food or food products that may contain lactose: milk from cows, sheep, goats. Dairy desserts, ice cream, butter, cheese, yoghurt, salad dressing, mayonnaise, chocolate, peanut butter, bread and other baked goods, processed meat and fish products, instant products, sweets, and additives containing lactose. | Lactose intolerance occurs in individuals who lack the enzyme lactase, which is needed to digest the milk sugar lactose. As the term suggests lactose intolerance is a food intolerance, not an allergy. Symptoms include flatulence and general discomfort. |

### In the club restaurant

### Which staff are impacted?

It is important to deliver training in allergens from a front of house perspective, and from the kitchen perspective, because both sets of staff will be impacted by the legislation. Training for staff needs to be built-in to everyday occurrences in the restaurant/food or catering operation.

Front of house – as an example: there will need to be a greater focus around cross-contamination. An example of this would be training staff not to put gluten-free bread on the same board as standard bread.

Back of house – in the kitchen – there are everyday occurrences such as making stocks for gravies that have a multitude of ingredients and vary from chef to chef and from one site to another.

So, it is vitally important that all staff develop an awareness of the ingredients of dishes and any allergenic ingredients are listed on menus. Where food is made to order chefs need to be aware of whether they are adding allergenic ingredients and what they might be.

### Create a plan

- Appoint an 'allergens champion' who will deal with your customers' queries about allergens and intolerances and educate other members of staff.
- Appoint a member of staff to take responsibility for overseeing how allergen information is expressed on menus and how signposting to members of staff who can give oral information should take place.
- This person should take responsibility for checking the ingredients used in menu items.
- Have a policy on how to deal with customers who suffer an allergic reaction.

### Providing allergen information

### Responsibilities

### Your responsibilities as a club operator

- To provide information on any of the 14 allergens
- To provide clear signposting to where this information can be obtained if specific allergen information is not provided upfront, for example, on a menu

- Information should be made available to all members of staff

**Customer responsibilities**

- To read the menu and inform a member of staff of any dietary requirements

- Check what allergens are in any dish they may order – bearing in mind they recipes and ingredients can change

- To take extra care in self-service cafes or restaurants or at self-service areas

**Requirement for non-pre-packed and pre-packed for direct sale foods**

Information on allergenic ingredients must be either:

- Written up front (for example on a menu or menu board) without the customer having to ask for information

- Sign-posted to where written information can be found or obtained

- Sign-posted to say that oral information can be obtained from a member of staff

- If information on allergenic ingredients is provided orally, this must be consistent and verifiable (i.e. a club must have processes in place to capture information from recipes or ingredients lists from products bought in, and make this available to staff)

It is important that customers with food allergies or intolerances can make informed choices when choosing products. All staff serving customers should be made aware of the potential risks to customers' health if they advise them incorrectly. A process must be in place to ensure that allergen information can be easily obtained and is accurate and consistent.

Customers are strongly advised to speak to staff regarding their allergy requirements. If a member of staff is unsure of the answer to a customer's question, they must ask somebody who knows.

Caterers can only use the phrase 'gluten-free' if they can demonstrate that, when tested, their product is 20 parts or less of gluten per million. They will also be required to demonstrate that any products claiming to be 'very low gluten' also comply with the legislation.

Caterers producing foods with no deliberate gluten containing ingredients, but due to the high risk of gluten cross-contamination, will be unable to label foods as 'gluten-free' or 'very low gluten'. Instead, if steps have been taken to control gluten cross-contamination, caterers will be able to indicate which foods do not contain gluten containing ingredients. This allows people with coeliac disease to make choices about the food they eat based on their individual levels of sensitivity.

## Tips on providing information

- When someone asks you if a food contains a particular ingredient, always check every time – never guess. If you are selling a food that contains one or more of the ingredients which can cause a problem, list them on the card, label, or menu – and make sure the information is accurate.

- Keep up-to-date ingredients information for any ready-made foods that you use (for example, a filling you put in a sandwich). The ingredients might be on the label or invoice.

- When you are making food, make sure you know what is in all the ingredients you use, including cooking oils, dressings, toppings, sauces, and garnishes.

- If you change the ingredients of a food, make sure you update your ingredients information and tell other staff about the change.

- If someone asks you to make some food for them that does not contain a particular ingredient, do not say yes unless you can make sure that absolutely none of that ingredient will be in the food.

- If you are making food for someone with an allergy, make sure work surfaces and equipment have been thoroughly cleaned. And wash your hands thoroughly before preparing that food.

- Make your menu easy for those with food allergies to understand. Provide full information.

## Recipe writing

**Ingredient statement** – list the ingredients used in each dish in their raw state and in the order of their quantity – from the highest to the lowest. Copy the ingredient list of every processed ingredient.

**Allergen statement** – you need to include the 14 food allergens, where they are present, on the menu or elsewhere.

**Checklist**

- Train staff in how to deal with food allergen enquiries from customers
- Ensure good kitchen practices and avoid cross-contamination
- Know the allergens in your menu items
- List any allergens on your menu or signpost on your menu to where customers can find out about them

## 9.0     How to Do Social Media

### Introduction

The use of social media platforms as a means of finding information and making decisions about where and what to eat and drink is now widespread. With more than 200 million posts tagged #food and 23 million with #drinks annually, food and beverage photos are easily some of the most popular types of content on Instagram. It is very likely that your customers are posting with or without your interaction.

When 88% of people are influenced by reviews and online comments, having an intentional digital strategy is important to your club and the promotion of its food and drinks offer. And it is not only younger consumers who use social media for these purposes.

If you're just getting started on your social media accounts, make sure pertinent information like your hours and contact information can be easily accessed on your profile – don't just put this on your website and passively hope it will generate responses from members, potential new members or their families.

### But, don't you have to be a geek to do this?

Perhaps you feel all this is a bit too difficult, or beyond your ability, needs to be done by an 'expert', a 'geek' – anyone aged under 12! If so, then use this 'How To' booklet as a template and instruction manual for an online solution provider. Whether it is DIY social media or you employ an outside provider, you can't afford not to engage with members, potential members and guests on social media – particularly if you want to attract and keep younger members.

## What is 'social media'?

### Old media

News, entertainment, and advertising reaches us through newspapers, magazines, TV, and the cinema. Content is controlled by a small group of individuals and organisations.

### New media

News, entertainment, and advertising can be made available to people through the Internet, but we would still need computer programmers to help us put our club's information online.

### Social media

New social media websites such as Facebook, Twitter, Instagram and YouTube now enable everyone with a computer, a tablet or a smartphone and Internet access to share news, information and promotional content with club members, friends, family, colleagues and the wider world.

### Save time and effort with social media management processes and tools

When you take the time to plan your social media in advance and invest in tools that help to save you time and effort, you are far more likely to achieve the positive results you hoped for.

Here are some top tips for getting organised with your social media:

- Invest in Social Media Management Tools

  - Setup an account with an online social media management solution provider (e.g. Hootsuite or SproutSocial). These free or low-cost solutions enable you to send social media messages to all your accounts and keep tabs on your customer communications across the channels from a single dashboard. These tools can be used on your PC or Mac and via an app on your smart phone.

- Plan in advance

  - Once every two weeks have a social media planning meeting or brainstorming session where you drum up ideas for new competitions, status updates, stories, and important promotional messages you want to share online. Then save time by scheduling your posts in advance using a social media management tool.

- Get your wider team involved in creating content

  - Do not burden one person with the sole responsibility of researching, creating, and sending out all your social media posts. When it comes to social media content creation, several heads are definitely better than one. Brainstorm ideas together at your club committee planning sessions and share the content creation tasks. For example, make different committee members responsible for photographing your weekly specials or for taking photographs at events.

## How social media can help your club

- Increase awareness of your club, its restaurant and other leisure facilities

  - When your social media fans and followers talk about, follow, like or share your social media profiles or content, potentially thousands more people will also see those public mentions of your club. Running a competition, making a special offer or advertising on social media also helps to increase awareness of your business.

- Create a buzz about your latest food and drink offer

  - You can post photographs, video, and engaging text updates on your social media accounts to draw attention to your latest menu items.

- Get customer feedback and insights

  - Today's customers love it when you ask for their opinion on your business. Use social media to find out what your members and guests think about your new drinks or menu items. Thinking of running a new darts, snooker, or live music evening? Why not ask your customers' first or invite them to suggest an alternative type of event for your club?

- Promote your events

  - Talk about the seasonal events you are hosting, e.g. Christmas, New Year's Eve, Halloween – it is not just for kids! Social media also provides a quick and easy way to promote your regular music gigs or football and other sports screenings.

- Update customers on your latest news

  - Have you refurbished your bar or restaurant area? Did you raise money for your favourite charity this month? Whatever your news, make sure to take a photograph and post it with a short news update on your social media accounts.

- Encourage sales with offers and specials
    - Fill those quiet periods by promoting specials or offers across your social media accounts.

- Make it easier for customers to recommend your business
    - Google+ and Facebook allow members and guests to star rate and review your club.
    - Google+ ratings are especially important as they can also help improve your search engine rating.
    - If you do not have any social media accounts, you are also far less likely to be mentioned and linked to in your customer's social media conversations.

- Promote job vacancies
    - Mention new job posts on your social media accounts and encourage your existing staff to share vacancy information with their friends and family.

- Connect with other businesses and your wider community
    - Win more friends and fans online when you rave about your top suppliers and name check other local businesses. People love to share positive comments about their business, so spread the love and you could end up with a win-win situation for both parties.

- Monitor your competitors
    - Keep a close eye on your competitors by following or reviewing their social media accounts on a regular basis.

- Build a customer database
    - Add a newsletter signup form to your Facebook page so you can build your customer database and stay in touch with your customers via email.

**Planning for social media success**

**What are your business objectives for using Social Media?**

Be clear about your club's objectives for using social media. If you know what you would like to achieve and you successfully communicate these objectives with your committee members and wider membership, you are far more likely to meet your targets.

Here are some example social media objectives that you could adapt for your club:

- Build a following of X on Twitter or win X new 'Likes' for our Facebook account in a given year

- Increase our regular Facebook 'Talking About This' number to 10% of our total Facebook Fans

- Increase awareness and ticket sales by X for a new events programme

- Improve your customer response rate on social media (set a target to reply to all customer messages within X hours)

- Increase awareness of a new cocktail line or Sunday lunch offer and help increase sales for this line item by X%

Also, work out how much time and money you are prepared to spend on your social media management each week. If you end up using your time and money in an unplanned way, it is likely that you will end up spending more and achieving less than you had hoped for.

## Present a strong brand image of your club

In today's world image is everything, so make sure your ACC brand logos, your club's logo, colours, and images are consistent across all your social media accounts.

Top social media branding tips:

- Use a square image for your Facebook page profile or Twitter profile photo that will be recognisable even when viewed as a small icon

- Use your Facebook timeline cover image or Twitter header image to suggest the mood or tone of your business

- Shorten your Facebook name at: www.facebook.com/username to create a friendly and short address that's easy to promote

- Use the same style of branded imagery across your chosen social media channels to make your brand appear strong and consistent

## Promote your social media accounts IN YOUR CLUB

Once your social media accounts are up and running, take every opportunity to promote them to your members and guests on notice boards, posters and beer mates for example.

## Promote your social media accounts ONLINE

Here are some popular ways to increase awareness of your social media channels online.

- Your website
    - Add links to your social media accounts on your homepage and on your 'contact us' page
    - Add Social Media share buttons on your website
- Your email newsletter
    - Use your newsletter to invite people to join you on Twitter, Facebook etc.
- Cross-promote on your social media accounts
    - Promote your Twitter on Facebook and Google+ and vice versa across all your accounts
- Mobile App
    - If you have created a mobile app for your business, invite customers to like you and share news via your app on Facebook, Twitter etc.

## Promote your social media by EMAIL

- Invite your email contacts to like your Facebook page
    - To import your email contacts from Outlook or another email service, go to your Facebook Admin panel, select 'Build Audience' > 'Invite Email Contacts'
    - Choose the email contacts option that suits you best. For example, to send an email to your Google Mail or Microsoft Outlook contacts, export your contacts first as a .csv file from your email software and then upload your contacts using the 'Browse' and 'Upload contacts' options shown on the right.
- Invite your email contacts to follow your Twitter account

- Login to your Twitter account and select '#Discover' > 'Find Friends'

- Search for your contacts using the Email service options provided by Twitter (Hotmail, Gmail etc.) or use the 'Invite friends via email' option which allows you to simply copy & paste in a list of comma separated emails and then send an invite directly from Twitter.

  For more information visit; https://support.twitter.com/groups/53-discover/topics/219-find-friends/articles/101002-finding-friends-using-an-email-address-book#

## Promote your social media accounts PAID FACEBOOK POSTS

- Use Facebook 'Boost Post' option to reach a wider audience

  - The Facebook 'boost post' option (which appears at the bottom of every one of your Facebook page posts) allows you to advertise to anyone who is liked your page and their friends on Facebook. With many Facebook posts being seen by only a fraction of the people who 'liked' a page, this is becoming an important way for many pubs, bars and restaurants to stay visible and get a return from their investment on their Facebook marketing.

  - If you want to reach a new target audience in your area, you can also reach people on Facebook through the 'Boost Post' targeting options shown on the right.

  - For more on the 'Boost Post' feature visit: https://www.facebook.com/help/547448218658012

## Create engaging social media content

- Follow these top tips to ensure your day-to-day social media content is well received.

  - Keep it short

  - Shorter posts on social media tend to get more engagement. For example, on Facebook posts between 100 and 250 characters (less than 3 lines of text) see about 60% more likes, comments and shares than longer posts.

- Do not just sell.

  - Find interesting news and stories to share with your customers

219

- When you do sell…

    - use a sociable tone, humour, or wit to make it more appealing

- Post images and photographs

    - Facebook users are up to 180% more likely to interact with an image as opposed to a text message so use images whenever possible.

- Encourage conversations

    - Ask questions. Get people to share their opinion. This works especially well with younger audiences.

- Be Current

    - Respond to the latest news, the weather and big events in your local area

- Create a social media buzz with competitions and prize draws

    - Many customers will jump on a chance to win a free meal or ticket to one of your special events so, if it is appropriate for your brand, include regular competitions and prize draws.

- Keep a consistent tone

    - Do not confuse your customers by changing your tone of language every other day or week. Work out what tone best represents your club's personality and stick to it.

**The rules on promoting alcohol via social media**

As on all other media channels, there are strict rules about promoting alcohol across the various social media channels. To make sure you stay on the right side of the law, make sure you:

- Act in compliance with all applicable laws and industry standards for each location that you are targeting.

- Do not target individuals below the legal drinking age.

- Do not imply that drinking alcohol can improve social, sexual, professional, intellectual, or athletic standing.

- Do not imply that drinking alcohol provides health or therapeutic benefits.

- Do not portray excessive drinking in a positive light or feature binge or competition drinking.

- Do not show alcohol being consumed in conjunction with the operation of machinery or a vehicle of any kind or the performance of any task requiring alertness or dexterity.

- Do not depict violent or degrading behaviour.

For more information on the terms of use regarding social media content and alcohol you can also check out the following links:

Twitter: https://support.twitter.com/articles/20170440-alcohol-content#

Facebook: https://www.facebook.com/help/358970040838616?sr=2&sid=0SxveRwqcj327EQQf

YouTube: https://support.google.com/adwordspolicy/answer/176005?hl=en&ref_topic=1310883

## Use hashtags to increase your visibility on social media

### What is a hashtag?

People search for #hashtags on various social media channels to see what people are saying about a particular subject. To join the conversation, you simply add that #hashtag to your message and it will join the stream with other posts on that subject.

### How do you create a hashtag?

You can turn any keyword or phrase into a hashtag by simply adding a # symbol at the start and by removing any spaces between words. Hashtags can be any length, but shorter ones work better.

### Where can you use a hashtag?

Hashtags are most popularly used on Twitter, Instagram and Pinterest and they are also starting to see more usage on Facebook.

### What hashtags should I use?

To learn how to use hashtags, watch out for #hashtags that are used by your customers or competitors and then think how you can include the popular ones in your tweets or posts. Topical and location hashtags seem to work best on Twitter. E.g. #6nations #twickers. On Instagram and Pinterest, use plenty of hashtag keywords to describe what you are talking about e.g. #sundayroast, #cocktails. You can also get creative and make up new ones just for fun.

## 1.0    USEFUL CONTACTS

Advisory, Conciliation and Arbitration Service
Euston Tower
286 Euston Road
London NW1 3DP
020 7210 3613
0300 123 1100 (helpline)
www.acas.org.uk

Companies House
Crown Way
Maindy
Cardiff   CF14 3UZ
02920 388 588
0870 333 3636 (contact centre)
www.companieshouse.gov.uk
email enquiries@companies-house.gov.uk

Home Office
Direct Communications Unit
2 Marsham Street
London SW1P 4DF
020 7035 4742

Financial Conduct Authority
12 Endeavour Square
London E20 1SN
0800 111 6768 or 0300 500 8082
Gambling Commission
Victoria Square House, Victoria Square
Birmingham  B2 4BP
0121 230 6666
www.gamblingcommission.gov.uk
email info@gamblingcommission.gov.uk

Greenock Accounting Centre (GAC)
Custom House, Custom House Quay
Greenock  PA15 1EQ
01475 881 431/434/435

PPL/PRS Limited
The Music Licence
Mercury Place
St. George's Street
Leicester LE 1 1QG
0800 072 0808
www.ppluk.com
email info@ppluk.com

Health & Safety Executive Books
(HSE Books)
18 Central Avenue
Norwich
NR7 0HR
0333 202 5020
www.hsebooks.com

Information Commissioner's Office
Wycliffe House
Water Lane
Wilmslow
Cheshire  SK9 5AF
0303 123 1113
www.ico.gov.uk
Data Protection Registrar (notifications)
email notification@ico.gsi.gov.uk

Local Government Association (LGA)
Local Government House
Smith Square
London  SW1P 3HZ
020 7664 3131
www.lga.gov.uk
email info@lga.gov.uk

Royal Institution of Chartered Surveyors
12 St George Street
London SW1P 3AD
021 7686 8555
www.rics.org
email contactrics@rics.org

## 2.0 INDEX